Contents

Introduction

Have you ever felt like skiing and snowboarding holidays belong to another world, a world that you're not quite sure how to break into? The world of winter sports is not an exclusive 'members only' club – these are activities that can be enjoyed by everybody, regardless of age or experience. They've also never been more accessible and more affordable. But if you're not lucky enough to have been before or have friends or family to show you the way, the first foray into this wintry world can be quite a daunting prospect. Where do you go? What clothes and equipment do you need? How much is it going to cost you? Should you ski or snowboard?

I have met many people who have never been on a skiing or snowboarding holiday, not because they don't want to, but because they don't know where to start; aware that they are missing out but frustrated at not knowing how to be part of it all. This book is a chance to demystify the world of winter sports holidays, opening the door for everyone to enjoy.

We're not going to teach you how to ski here, and we're not going to teach you how to snowboard – there are professionally trained instructors who can do that far better in practice than I can on paper – but what this book will do is prepare you for your first venture into the winter mountains. Where to go, when to go, what to bring with you and what to expect when you get out there; pitfalls to avoid, helpful hints to make things better and top tips on what and what not to do.

Skiing and snowboarding will open your eyes to a whole new side of life, and a whole new set of addictive emotions. Adrenalin like you've never experienced, the freedom of movement, breathtaking views and awe-inspiring mountains, feeling alive and being invigorated. So what's stopping you? Come on, there's no time like the present – read this book, and then get out there and organise your first winter ski holiday. I guarantee that once you've got a taste, you won't look back!

Chapter One

Beginner's Skiing

The skiing bug is a cunning little thing. It will creep up on you when you least expect it and give you a nibble that at first seems relatively small, but like all good biters the itch will grow with time. We all know what you've got to do with an itch…scratch it! But the more you scratch it, the itchier it gets!

Skiing is addictive. It's the joy of movement and the pleasure of flying down a mountain feeling free, adrenalin surging through your veins. It's the wonderful environment you're in – if it wasn't for skiing, most of us would never have the opportunity to get up into such beautiful high mountains, with their rocky ridges, deep valleys and snow covered peaks. And then there's the sociability of it all – laughter with friends, steaming cups of hot chocolate around open fires, that well-earned beer at the end of the day that's never tasted so good. Or, alternatively, the poetic solitude of winging it downhill, with nothing but you and the mountains to interrupt.

There's no sex or age barrier – young and old, male and female. Families can enjoy together, and if you didn't learn when you were younger then learn now – there's nothing stopping you. Anyone who's normally active can get pleasure out of skiing – don't be intimidated by pictures of extreme skiers hurtling down vertical gullies; the mountain provides us with a real mix of different gradients, from the flat to the gently sloping, and every gradient from there to vertical.

'Skiing is addictive. It's the joy of movement and the pleasure of flying down a mountain feeling free, adrenalin surging through your veins.'

Looking back

Skiing first originated thousands of years ago as a mode of transport in northern Europe, to get around in flat, snowy countries, such as Norway, during their long, cold winters. The skis used at this time were primarily Nordic skis, a form of which is still used today in cross-country skiing. Skiing was then adopted by the army for use in the winters, and soon after followed the first ski races.

The use of ski poles developed from walking poles used for balance when snowshoeing. Snowshoes enable you to walk on snow without sinking up to your knees – making it less exhausting and far more practical to get around. Before the development of the first skis, these would have been the principle means of getting around, although a lot slower. We'll look at both snowshoeing and cross-country skiing in more detail in chapter 9.

Downhill skiing evolved from Nordic skiing comparatively recently. In the 19th century, a Norwegian developed a pair of ski bindings that attached your foot to the ski more securely and enabled you to ski more aggressively, with less risk of losing your bindings. He also started using skies that were shorter and more shapely to enable him to have more control on steeper gradients.

Another pioneer then developed even firmer bindings, making it easier for the skier to turn more effectively, and gradually these evolved into the downhill skis that we use today. Over the years skis have become shorter and shorter and have developed from being made out of a solid piece of wood to being made from a composition of different materials, including fibreglass – although, many do still have a lightweight wooden core.

> 'As a beginner, there's no avoiding the undeniable fact that you have to start at the beginning – don't turn up to your first lesson expecting to have mastered it by the end of the day.'

Beginners

As a beginner, there's no avoiding the undeniable fact that you have to start at the beginning – don't turn up to your first lesson expecting to have mastered it by the end of the day. But don't get frustrated – as an adult, it may have been a long time since you were a beginner at something. Stick at it and you'll get there – it will be well worth the time invested.

This book is not going to teach you how to ski – you're far better off booking a lesson with a qualified ski instructor, either at an artificial slope in the UK (see chapter 6) or at a resort.

However, there are a few top tips that I can give you here which will enable you to turn up to day one feeling more confident.

Gravity is an undeniable fact, so learning to stop and learning to turn are the two key skills needed in order to stay in control. Don't be afraid, or embarrassed, to fall – falling is part of the process; everyone does it, even the experts.

Carrying your skis

The very first skill to learn, however, is how to carry your skis from the hire shop to the piste. Now, you may laugh that I've brought this up, but there is nothing more frustrating than carrying skis incorrectly – they bump and slide against each other, bang into your head, separate, fall, trip you up and knock passers-by. A few simple tips though can solve this problem. Ensure the skis are both pointing in the same direction, with their bases together. Then with your skis together in this fashion, lift them onto one shoulder, with the tips pointing down towards the floor in front of you and the tail end up in the air over your shoulder. If you struggle to get the skis to stay together, you can buy a small Velcro strap to tie around them to stop them from sliding apart, or fashion one easily enough with a rubber band.

Putting the skis on

So, now we've managed to actually get to the slope, what next? Let's put the skis on.

Place each ski separately, base down, on a flat area of snow. Place your ski poles squarely on either side of you – you might want to lean on them for balance. Ensure the backs of the bindings are pushed down. Clear the snow off the base of your boots and then, one foot at a time, push the toe of your ski boot into the front of the binding and then press the heel down so it clips in place. Finally, take hold of your poles and put your hand up through the wrist strap and down, so you're holding the pole's grip. You're now ready to go!

If putting on your skis while standing on a slope, there are a few things to think about. Make sure you position your skis so they're lying across the slope, not pointing down at an angle – you'll find yourself sliding off before you're ready, and nobody wants that. Always put the downhill ski on first (the ski lower down the slope) – this makes you more stable when putting on your second ski.

Stance

Dos

Make sure your weight is distributed evenly between the skis. Relax your arms and have your feet at a comfortable distance apart. Flex your knees and make sure they are not touching – being 'knock-kneed' won't help. Bend your ankles forward and keep your head up (for an image, please refer to the parallel stance on page 13).

Don'ts

The two main errors that people make when first learning to ski are either leaning back or standing up too straight. Relaxing into a flexed knee will make it a lot easier to control the ski.

Moving forward

To gain some forward momentum on flat ground, slide your feet forward one at a time, in short gliding steps, keeping the ski flat on the snow and avoiding lifting the ski in an exaggerated fashion into the air.

When you begin to go on slopes that have some downwards gradient, the main skill to master is turning and, of course, stopping. The reason why we turn on skis is to control our speed and our descent. If you were to just point downhill and make a beeline straight for the base of the mountain, you would pick up more and more speed and not have much control over your skis or yourself.

'When you begin to go on slopes that have some downwards gradient, the main skill to master is turning.'

Skis are designed specifically to move in a curve. If you look at the shape of them, pretty much every ski is narrower at the waist and wider at the tips.

A ski has two sharp edges and a flat base. Putting pressure on one edge of a ski will cause it to arc out and turn in that direction. Shifting the pressure to the other edge of the ski will cause it to arc and turn the other way.

Skiing is effectively a series of connected curves. When you first start, you will practise wider turns. But as your confidence and control of the skis increases, you will practise narrower, tighter and more direct turns. Turning should be a smooth arcing action, not a sudden jerky movement.

Tip

Think of your legs as springs – flexing and extending at the knee to absorb the bumps of the slope, and pushing and lifting you through your turns.

Snow plough

When first starting out, you will learn a technique called 'snow ploughing'. This is a stance where you form a triangle shape with your skis – with the tips pointing in towards each other in front of you and the tails pointing out behind you. Skiing with your skis in the snow plough position is a great way to gain confidence and feel comfortable on your skis without picking up too much speed.

Start off snow ploughing without poles. This will help you find your centre of balance on the skis and learn the correct stance without relying on your poles to steady you.

When you're confident in turning in the snow plough position, it's time to learn how to do parallel turns.

Snow plough stance

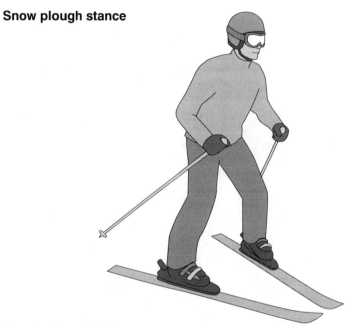

Parallel turning

This is the main technique that as a skier you are aiming to master.

The parallel ski stance is how it sounds: both skis parallel to one another, with the tips pointing in the same direction and skis no more than shoulder width apart.

It is here that the principle of turning by shifting your weight from edge to edge really comes into practice.

▪ Start traversing across the piste. When ready to turn, shift your weight to the outer edge of your downhill ski and, looking in the direction that you aim to travel in, follow the arc round that this ski takes, crossing the fall line, until you are facing in the other direction. (The fall line is the direct route down the slope.)

▪ To stop the turning momentum, lift and release the pressure from this ski.

▪ When you're ready to turn again, increase the pressure on the other ski

Parallel stance

(which is now your downhill ski), pushing down on the outside edge, forcing the ski into an arcing turn across the fall line, until you're once again facing the other way.

- Make sure you maintain a good stance throughout the turn, not allowing your shoulders to turn uphill, or one shoulder to 'trail' behind. This will make the turning movement awkward and difficult to carry out, reducing your control over the skis.

- Keep your skis apart and try not to cross the tips.

- Your ski poles can help you in the turn, propelling you and giving you a point to pivot around.

> **Tip**
>
> Think about where you want to turn, avoiding turning on top of a bump or other awkward feature.

Controlling your speed and stopping

If at any point you wish to check your speed or stop, the 'power slide' is a useful tool to have in your box of tricks.

This is where the skier pivots their skis directly beneath them, pushing hard down and into the snow. This will cause the skis to slide sideways, scraping across the snow. The friction this creates acts as a break or, if extra pressure is exerted, stops the forward momentum altogether.

Skiing in different conditions

Moguls

Moguls are domes of snow or lumps and bumps on a piste – these are sometimes quite large and can completely cover the piste. They are caused by many skiers all turning in the same place, gradually wearing the snow down in some areas and not in others. They are particularly prevalent on pistes that are poorly or irregularly groomed (the resort staff groom, or maintain, the pistes at night with machines, to keep the snow in good condition), and/or when there is a lack of fresh snow. If you find yourself on a moguled slope, time your turns so you turn around the moguls, not on top of them. The key to 'dominating' moguls is to do shorter, rhythmic turns, especially if the moguls are evenly spaced.

Powder

Powder snow is the soft, sometimes very deep, snow that hasn't been packed down by the pisting machines, which are often referred to as 'piste bashers'.

When skiing in powder snow, shift your body weight back a bit from your normal stance. By leaning back further than you normally would, you're keeping the tips of your skis from digging into the soft snow, helping the skis to remain on top of the snow.

In powder, movements need to be exaggerated in order to have the same effect as on piste. When turning, really exaggerate the motion, bending down low before the turn, and then really lift your weight up as you go through the turn. The result of this is to lift your skis up out of the snow, enabling you to turn on top of the soft snow rather than trying to move the skis through it.

This also applies in slushy snow. Slushy snow is sometimes found at the end of the season when temperatures are rising and the snow is melting. Although very different to powder snow, the technique of keeping your skis up out of the slush, therefore increasing the ease at which they can be manoeuvred, is similar to powder.

Ice

The key to skiing on ice is to have very sharp edges to your skis, and then to really put as much pressure on them as possible when crossing an icy patch. The sharp edges bite into the ice, stopping your skis from sliding away from under you.

Clothing and equipment for skiing

You'll be relieved to know that fashion has come a long way over the past 10 years. Whether you're a skier, snowboarder or spectator, at the time of writing the fashion for separate jacket and loose-fitting trousers rules. The level of bagginess of said attire is at the owner's discretion, but there is now no excuse to be seen up the mountain in tight fitting Lycra ski trousers! But that said, fashions change, and in 50 years time we could all be wearing space suits, so keep your ear to the ground.

The basic clothing you need for skiing is outlined in chapter 3; however, some main items of equipment that you will need are listed here.

Ski boots

Ski boots are made up of two parts – the inner and the outer. The outer is a rigid plastic shell that attaches securely to the ski, and the inner is a softer layer that fits closely to your foot, providing support and insulation.

When first trying on a pair of ski boots, don't be put off by the fact that it can be quite a struggle sometimes to get your foot in. The boot is very supportive around the ankle, preventing you from rolling on or breaking your ankle. They are meant to be a snug fit.

Once your foot is inside the boot and it's fully done up, it is important that your toes aren't curled against the end. You will not be able to get a good feel for whether the boot fits correctly sitting down, so it's worth standing up and flexing the knees, bending the ankle forward, mimicking the position you will adopt when on skis. In this position you should be able to wiggle your toes.

It's also worth checking, once again only when the boot is fully done up, how much heel lift you have. A bit of heel lift is fine, but if you can lift your heel up out of the foot area towards the ankle then the boot is too big for you. Don't be nervous to ask the shop assistant if you can try a different size, as there is nothing more effective at taking away the pleasure of a day's skiing than painful feet.

Modern ski boots are done up with a series of clips, which pull together the two sides of the boot, and can be tightened or loosened individually to suit.

We will discuss buying your own equipment in more detail in chapter 7. However, when you do get to the stage of wanting to purchase your own ski equipment, the boots are the most important things to start with. Many hire shops these days are excellent and stock good quality equipment, but hire boots will have had a lot of differently shaped feet in them during their life, and consequently the inners are pushed and pulled in all different directions and can lose their shape.

'Stretch pants – the garment that made skiing a spectator sport.'

Author Unknown.

Skis

When I first started skiing, the test for whether a pair of skis were the correct length for you was to stand upright with your arm stretched up above your head to see if the top of the skis touched your hand – how times have changed!

Downhill skis are now much shorter, and therefore easier to control. The exact length of ski you use is based on the ratio between your weight and height. Don't worry though, you won't be expected to work this out for yourself. The ski technician in the hire shop will tell you what length ski is right for you, based not just on your height and weight, but also what type of skiing you like to do.

There are a variety of different shapes of ski available:

- A general all-purpose ski, which is what most people need, is slightly wider at both ends and narrower in the middle. This is the basic shape for all modern downhill skis. This shape aids the ski in turning and makes it easier to control.

- Skis with an exaggerated narrow waist and wider ends are designed specifically for carving – which means focusing on doing very defined turns down the mountain.

- Skis that are extra wide are designed for skiing off piste. They have a larger surface area, so are easier to use in powder as they float on top of the snow.

- Skis with an upturned tip at both ends are designed for freestyle – the upturned tail enables you to ski backwards, as well as forwards, without the tail of the ski digging into the snow. This means the skier can do jumps, go in the halfpipe, and pretty much do all the tricks that a snowboarder can – even more, some skiers would argue. Freestyle or twin tip skis tend to be shorter, as they spin in the air better, compared to skis designed for bombing down pistes and skiing fast and straight, which tend to be a bit longer.

It's important you let the hire shop know what level of skier you are, as more advanced skis are a lot stiffer and need to be ridden more aggressively to get the best out of them – these are more suited to faster, steeper skiing.

Beginner skis are softer and don't need to be ridden so hard. They are much more forgiving and more suitable for entry level.

'It's important to let the hire shop know what level of skier you are, as more advanced skis are a lot stiffer and need to be ridden more aggressively to get the best out of them – these are more suited to faster, steeper skiing.'

Bindings

Modern bindings are attached to each ski. They are designed to both hold your foot securely in place on the ski and to release your foot if a hard twisting pressure is exerted, to avoid injury should you fall. This is a very important function of the bindings, so don't be concerned when you see the ski technician in the hire shop checking that your boot does twist out of the binding.

Bindings are easy to put on. Simply step into them, toe first. The toe area of your ski boot is designed to push neatly into the front of the ski binding. The back of the binding is a lever which clips into place when the heel of the ski boot is pushed down, securing the boot on the ski. In order to take your skis off, simply compress this lever at the back of the binding and the boot will be released. The bindings are adjustable to fit different foot sizes, and your weight will also be taken into consideration to ensure the boot is released successfully from the binding – a heavier skier will exert more pressure on the binding than a lighter skier.

Poles

Ski poles are intended to provide balance and stabilisation. When you first start learning, your instructor may make you ski without poles, so you can get used to the ski before another element is introduced. However, as you progress

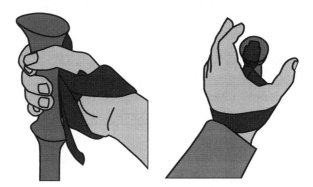

Holding your ski pole

you will find ski poles invaluable – for planting and pushing, for propelling you around a turn, for helping to push you along in flatter areas or when extra speed is required and, most importantly, for poking people in lift queues!

Poles come in a variety of different lengths to suit all heights of skier. Hold your arms out in front of you, bent at right angles to your body, with your elbows in by your waist. Where your hands are is where the handles of your poles should be.

As mentioned previously, the ski pole will have a wrist strap. The correct way to hold it is to put your hand up through this strap and then down around the handle, with the strap held between hand and the ski pole.

Summing Up

- If struggling to carry your skis, strap them together with a Velcro tie, or home made equivalent.

- Don't remain seated when trying on ski boots – stand up and flex your knees, as if you are on skis. Don't be afraid to ask to try on different sizes.

- Check there's not lots of snow stuck to the bottom of your boots when putting your skis on.

- When skiing, the most important thing to remember is: bend your knees, bends your knees, bend your knees!

Chapter Two

Beginner's Snowboarding

Snowboarding is liberating; it's freeing and designed for playing!

Snowboarding is for all to enjoy, no matter what your age. There's no time like the present to take a sideways look at the world, so stop procrastinating, stop talking yourself out of it, dust off your excitement receptors, and give it a go.

Looking back

Snowboarding is a comparatively young sport. It has evolved in less than 100 years from a child's toy to one of the most popular winter sports there is.

The first snowboard was developed back in 1929 when a man called M J Burchett took a plank of plywood and tried to strap his feet to it with some clothesline and horse reins (not to be recommended!).

Around 30 years later, a young surfer called Sherman Poppen made a gift of two skis strapped together for his daughter to play in the snow with. The idea was such a hit with the neighbourhood that one year later it was put into production and sold as the 'snurfer'. Despite the dodgy name, the first commercial snowboard was born!

The idea was picked up by Jake Burton, a young student during the 70s, who further developed the concept, experimenting with new designs and materials. Gradually, over the next decade, snowboarding spread in popularity across the US and eventually into Europe.

The design continued to evolve, including more structured bindings and metal edges, making snowboards easier to ride. In the early days, many ski resorts banned snowboarding on their slopes because of the bad reputation it had acquired among traditional winter sports enthusiasts, due to being associated with young and reckless surfers.

'Snowboarding is liberating; it's freeing and designed for playing! Snowboarding is for all to enjoy, no matter what your age.'

However, attitudes have changed, along with the demographic of snowboarders, which is now no longer dominated by young males. Rather it is a complete mix of ages and sex, and both skiers and snowboarders now happily enjoy the mountain side-by-side.

Essential equipment

When first learning, it's not necessary to buy your own equipment right from the outset – boots, boards and bindings can all be easily hired in the ski resort at the start of your holiday.

Boots

When it comes to equipment, one of the biggest plus points about snowboarding is the footwear. No squeezing your feet into plastic vices required here, snowboarding boots don't need the rigidity that ski boots do, as snowboard bindings provide a lot of the support instead. Consequently, the boots do not have the hard plastic shell of ski boots; they're softer, infinitely more comfortable and a lot easier to put on. They are fully insulated, keeping your feet warm (although a good pair of thick socks is advisable), and are usually tightened around the foot using a lacing system. As with ski boots, snowboard boots have an inner and an outer boot, which can be tightened separately, offering you more control over the lacing and therefore the fit and comfort levels.

Snowboards

Snowboards come in many different shapes and sizes. Contrary to popular belief, the length of board you use is based more on your weight than your height – the heavier you are, the longer the board you will need. Some boards are unisex, but in general, boards are separated into men's and women's. As well as being longer, due the obvious difference in rider weight, men's boards also tend to be wider to accommodate men's bigger feet. Any good shop assistant will be able to advise you on the best board size for you, and you'll soon get to know the length of board that you prefer.

Now, let's take a look at the different styles of board:

- Freeride boards are designed to be ridden both on and off piste, and are aimed at people who want to spend the day exploring the mountain – sometimes referred to as 'all mountain' or 'all terrain' boards. They tend to be longer than freestyle boards, for riding fast and straight.

- Freestyle boards are designed for riders whose main aim is to be hitting jumps, grinding rails, falling over in the halfpipe and spending time in the snow park. These boards tend to be shorter than freeride boards, making them more manoeuvrable and easier to spin.

- Carving boards differ in shape to the other boards mentioned here – although they're still curved at the nose, they're straight across at the tail and have a deeper side-cut. They are designed specifically with carving downhill in mind, and stiffer ski-like boots are worn with them. This is the least common type of board seen on the mountain.

Bindings

So, now all you're missing is a pair of bindings to attach your feet to your board. The most common style of binding consists of a solid backboard, a strap that tightens across the toe area and one that tightens around the ankle. They are generally made from plastic and the straps tighten with a ratchet-style system. Bindings come in various different sizes, so make sure your bindings are wide enough to fit your boots and not too long so that they hang over the front of your board.

There is another style of binding not commonly used – the 'clip-in' binding. After a brief surge of popularity (based more on novelty factor than anything else), they are rarely seen these days. They were designed to be quicker and easier to put on, requiring a special boot to accompany them that has a clip-in section in the sole. The boot then clips into the setting attached to the board. The main problems with this style of binding is that firstly the clip-in area both on the board and on the sole of the boot can get frozen up with snow and ice when you take your board off, making it difficult to re-attach the board when you're ready to head off again. There's nothing worse than having to remove your glove to clear a snow-clogged binding when it's -10°C! Secondly, due to the lack of support that a clip-in binding provides compared to a regular strap-in binding, you can feel less in tune with the board when riding.

I would advise you stick to the regular strap-in binding set-up.

Bindings from equipment hire shops in resort will often have a leash on the front binding that attaches to your leg. This is useful when first learning, as it stops the board from sliding off down the mountain without you – a helpful feature if you accidentally let go of it while strapping in!

Best foot forward

'Now you've got your board, bindings and boots, it's time to piece it all together. The first decision you need to make is which is your lead foot.'

Now you've got your board, bindings and boots, it's time to piece it all together. The first decision you need to make is which is your lead foot. This is the foot that you choose to have at the front of the board, in the direction that you wish to travel. If you've ever done any other board sports, for example surfing or skateboarding, then you'll use the same foot forward for snowboarding. If not, there are different ways that people suggest you work it out. Some people just intuitively know, others say if someone gives you a shove from behind, the foot you put forward to steady yourself is your lead foot. But, ultimately, it's whichever foot feels most natural.

The most common foot to have forward is the left foot. This is referred to as being 'regular'. If you feel more comfortable with your right foot forward, this is referred to as being 'goofy' (but worry not – this title is not intended to double-up as a character assassination!). Neither set-up is better than the other; it's just what feels the most comfortable for you. If you're struggling to decide, try having your left foot forward for the day. If after riding for a bit you naturally want to ride with your right foot forward, then it's easy to switch your bindings around.

Left and right bindings are both attached to the board independently and can be adjusted separately. Your bindings should be attached to your board a minimum of shoulder width apart, with your front foot pointing slightly forward and your back foot at a neutral angle. As you improve, you can increase the angle that your feet are turned apart from each other, making it easier to do tricks and ride facing in the opposite direction (referred to as riding switch or fakey). The recommended angles to start with are your front foot at 15° and your back foot at 0°. There are clear markings on your bindings to help you set this up. If hiring a board, the shop assistant will do all of this for you.

One point to note, if the time comes when you decide to buy your own board and bindings, make sure the attachment plates on your bindings are compatible with your board. Some manufacturers, annoyingly, differ – presumably to encourage you to buy both board and bindings from the same brand.

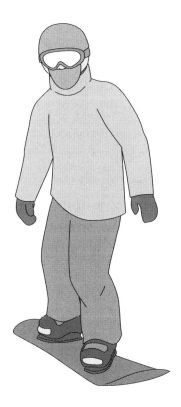

Regular footed snowboarder

Goofy footed snowboarder

Clothing

The main clothing items (trousers, jacket and gloves) are the same for all the different winter mountain sports discussed in this book, and are covered in more detail in chapter 3.

However, there are a couple of things worth considering when heading out on your board. Regardless of the weather, it's advisable to wear goggles rather than glasses. You're very physical when riding a board, particularly when learning, and part of the fun when learning is that you're likely to fall over a lot and be up and down regularly. The last thing you want is your sunglasses falling off all the time or, even worse, breaking while on your face. While we're on the subject of falling over, it's possible to buy wrist guards to protect your wrists during those early days when learning. These aren't essential, but if nothing else, they provide a good confidence boost for nervous beginners. A helmet is definitely recommended – you don't have to hit your head hard to do serious damage.

Hitting the slopes

Don't let the previous onslaught of information about equipment baffle you. These are useful pointers to refer back to as you gain more experience and, as with all action sports, playing around with the equipment and settings becomes part of the addiction. However, as previously mentioned, when you're a beginner, the hire shop will sort all this out for you.

If you've never been snowboarding before, it's advisable to have a couple of lessons at your local artificial ski slope, of which there are many around the country (see chapter 6 for more information). Due to being made from real snow rather than matting, they are a great place to master the real basics and get you used to the sensation of being on a board on snow. By having a few lessons before you get out to a resort, you leapfrog that first stage of learning and can enjoy your holiday to the full.

So, how do you do it then?

Here are a few pointers to get you started.

Putting on the board

When first putting on your board, make sure you're on a flat surface. Then before you do anything, attach your leg leash. Not all boards have a leg leash, but many beginner hire boards come with one attached to the front binding. This can prove very handy for stopping boards flying off down the mountain when accidentally let go of by fumbling hands. Then, sitting down, strap your front foot into the binding. The bindings should be tight, but not so tight that they stop circulation.

As you don't have ski poles to push you along on flat areas, the easiest way to move about on the flat is with your front foot strapped in, and your back foot (not strapped in) pushing you along.

When you reach an area of downhill gradient, sit down, strap your back foot in, and you're ready to go.

Basic riding stance

- Most of your weight (approx 80%) should be over your front foot rather than your back foot.

- Bend at the knees, not at the waist – your knees act as shock absorbers.

- Stand parallel with the board and then turn your hips, shoulder and head slightly in the direction of travel.

- Keep your head up and your eyes looking ahead rather than down at your board.

- To begin with, keep your arms out stretched to help with balance.

- Most importantly, relax! This will make everything so much easier.

Balancing exercises

Once both feet are strapped in, it's worth familiarising yourself with the feel of your board and getting used to having both feet strapped to it.

Standing on a flat area of snow, try jumping up and down, then leaning heavily on each foot in turn. This really shows how the board moves and flexes. Also, try leaning heavily on your toe edge (the side of the board that your toes are pointing) and then your heel edge (the side of the board that your heels are pointing to), to familiarise yourself with the movement.

Stopping and controlling speed

In order to stop your board or to check your speed, you need to use the edges of the board as brakes.

When you lean onto one edge of the board, increasing the angle that it digs into the snow and lifting the other edge, the increased pressure exerted into the snow will result in increased friction. This forces the board to slow down or stop, depending on how heavily this pressure is applied.

Two essential skills worth learning that will help you control your speed are 'side slipping' and 'the falling leaf'.

Side slipping – this is great for checking speed on steeper slopes and for getting out of awkward spots. Stand with the board across the slope and the toe edge digging into the snow, facing into the piste. Relax and keep your weight equal over both feet, using your arms for balance.

Gradually, reduce the angle that your toe edge is directed into the slope, by lowering your heel edge. As this angle reduces, the friction will also reduce, and gradually the board will begin to slide down the slope. You can control the speed of this sliding descent by increasing or decreasing the angle of your toe edge. Once you've got the hang of doing this on your toe edge, turn around and try it on your heel edge, facing outwards.

Once you're happy with this, start shifting your weight onto one foot and then the other, and experience the board traversing across the slope.

Falling leaf – this is a great technique to use on tricky terrain, or for avoiding obstacles in your path. Stand with your board across the slope and follow the same motion described above, putting the majority of your weight on your front foot so that you traverse across the slope. As the nose of the board moves down the slope, transfer your weight back to the other foot and traverse in the other direction. Keep on repeating and you'll move down the piste in a motion similar to that of a falling leaf. This can be done on both your toe and your heel edge.

'Unfortunately, as a novice snowboarder there's no avoiding it – you are going to fall, regularly in fact! But don't get disheartened or frustrated – it is a part of the learning process that everyone goes through.'

How to fall

Unfortunately, as a novice snowboarder there's no avoiding it – you are going to fall, regularly in fact! But don't get disheartened or frustrated – it is a part of the learning process that everyone goes through. So here are a few tips to help you minimise any potential injuries:

- If falling forwards, try not to use your hands to stop the fall – instead, fall onto your clenched fists or forearms. Wrists tend to twist and sprain easily.

- If falling backwards, try to relax. You're more likely to jar your neck or back if you're tense and rigid.

- If falling on steeper ground, dig the edge of your board into the snow – this will act as a break to stop you from sliding too far down the piste.

- If you're struggling, or worried, it might be worth investing in wrist guards or kneepads.

Turning

A snowboard has a flat base with sharp edges. The basic board shape is narrower at the waist and wider at the ends. This is designed so that when moving forwards and pressure is exerted onto one of the edges, the board turns in an arcing curve.

- To initiate a turn, start off on your toe edge, facing into the slope. Think about your posture – knees bent, head up and shoulders, head and waist turned slightly in the direction of travel. Put approximately 80% of your weight onto your front foot, so you are traversing across the piste, as explained above.

- Then, with your arms out for balance, lean onto your heel edge, simultaneously pointing your forward arm in the direction you wish to travel – this will encourage you to move your body round in the direction of the turn, and with your weight on the heel edge, your board will curve round to follow.

- Once around the turn, extend your body upwards to release the pressure on your board, enabling you to then sink back down with your knees, weight on your front foot. You should now be facing in the other direction, toes pointing down the slope.

- When ready to initiate the next turn, repeat the above – this time putting your weight on your toe edge, pointing where you plan to turn to with your forward arm and arcing the board round.

Most beginners initially find it easier to turn on their heel edge. But practice makes perfect and you'll soon be linking turns all the way down.

Riding in powder snow

Snowboards are at their best in powder snow; for me this is what it's all about! Their large surface area means they just float along on top of the powder, and whereas skiing in powder snow is an advanced skill, snowboarding in powder can be picked up pretty quickly.

The main point to note when riding in powder is to ignore the on-piste rules of putting your weight onto your front foot. Instead, lean back onto your back foot – this will lift the nose of the board up, preventing it from digging into the soft snow and sending you flying.

The premise of turning remains the same, shifting your weight from one edge of your board to the other. However, it's easier to do shorter rather than long turns in powder. If you're riding in soft, slushy snow (melting snow), it also helps to put more weight onto your back foot, once again preventing the nose of the board from digging into the snow.

The snow park

Many resorts now have snow parks. The main features you will find in the snow park are kickers (wedge shaped mounds of snow for jumping off), with a run up, take-off ramp and landing. These come in a variety of sizes – from small to scary!

Many parks will also have a number of 'rails', which is a spin off from the world of skateboarding. There are also 'boxes', which are like bench seats. The aim of these is to time the approach well and slide the board at various angels over the rail or box.

The halfpipe is another snow park favourite. This is a semi circle cut out into the snow. Riders travel back and forth, from side to side of the pipe. They perform tricks as they jump up out of the edges, turning in the air so they're ready to come back into the pipe, and then ride to the other side and repeat.

Summing Up

- Decide whether you are regular footed (left foot forward) or goofy (right foot forward).

- Bend your knees and look in the direction you want to go.

- When learning to turn, don't be afraid of picking up speed when facing down the fall line – you're not going as fast as you think you are.

- Always sit to the side of the piste, so you're out of the way of oncoming traffic.

Chapter Three

Clothing

Every sport has its essential items, its technical clothing – and its fashions – and skiing and snowboarding are no different.

Skiing and snowboarding fashions have been through a whole host of different incarnations – from the daring and the disastrous, to the understated and the over-the-top; tight Lycra, all-in-one suits, fluorescent colours and matching patterns from head to toe. You can even buy hats with built-in headphones, fur-lined jackets and gold plated goggles if you so choose. Gucci have their own branded snowboards and Armani have their own ski clothing collection.

However, before your palms start to sweat at the prospect of having to spend ridiculous amounts of money, only to look, well, ridiculous, then worry not – dressing the part doesn't have to cost you the earth. Most people don't wear bizarre designer gear, but rather technical clothing made by experts in the field.

This is an area that can't be bypassed in favour of a hotchpotch of old clothes from the back of your wardrobe, with a pac-a-mac thrown over the top. In order for you to enjoy your holiday to the full, it's essential you go prepared – turning up and trying to wing it just doesn't work. Mountain weather can be harsh and unforgiving, but with a bit of common sense and forward planning, you'll be gliding along feeling warm, smug and having the time of your life.

Specialist stores such as Snow+Rock and Ellis Brigham both stock an extensive range of skiing and snowboarding clothing, both in style and price. For a real bargain, Decathlon sell their own-brand ski jackets and trousers (winter stock usually arrives in stores around October time). These are perfect if you're going on your first trip and don't want to commit to more expensive clothing, in case it turns out to be your last trip! Although, you do get what you pay for – and cheaper clothing won't be as effective or last as long.

'Every sport has its essential items, its technical clothing – and its fashions – and skiing and snowboarding are no different.'

If on a budget, it's also well worth having a look in TK Maxx, as some great deals on respectable brands can often be found here.

If you really don't want to shell out on clothing for your first trip then there are a growing number of suppliers who hire out the main clothing essentials – jacket and trousers. A good starting point is www.edge2edge.co.uk.

Whether skiing, snowboarding, sledging or drinking hot chocolate in a mountain restaurant, there are certain basic items that are required.

Jacket

This is one of the main items of clothing needed to keep you both warm and dry. Your jacket must be windproof and waterproof. Some jackets include a lot of insulation, meaning only light layers are needed beneath. Other jackets are thinner with less insulation, meaning you may need to layer up with a fleece or thicker jumper depending on the weather. It is an advantage to have a hood on your jacket – if you get caught in a snowstorm, this will provide you with extra protection.

Things to look for when buying a jacket are the seams – make sure they're sealed and waterproof – and the zip should be protected beneath a flap so it doesn't freeze. It's also useful to have lots of pockets to stash suntan cream, hat, money, phone, lip balm, iPod and anything else you want to take out on the slopes.

Most jackets designed with skiing or snowboarding in mind will have a built-in 'snow skirt'. This is an internal layer of material that does up tightly around the waste, stopping unwanted snow from going up the jacket, or the jacket being pushed up under your arm pits if you have a tumble. When trying on a jacket, make sure it's large enough for you to move your arms around freely and to fit extra layers beneath.

To access ski lifts, it's necessary to show or scan your ski pass at the entry gate. Modern lifts are fitted with scanners, which are traditionally on the left as you pass through the gate. In response to this, a lot of modern jackets have a pocket on the left-hand side especially designed to house your ski pass – this is a useful feature.

'Things to look for when buying a jacket are the seams – make sure they're sealed and waterproof – and the zip should be protected beneath a flap so it doesn't freeze.'

Trousers

As with the jacket, your trousers also need to be waterproof and insulated. If you remember only one thing after reading this book then it should be this: never, ever think you can save the cost of buying ski trousers by wearing your old denim jeans! It has to be one of the most miserable items of clothing to wear when wet and cold, and you'd be surprised how many novices try and get away with it.

Investing in a proper pair of ski or snowboarding trousers is worthwhile. This is for a number of reasons – your trousers will experience a lot of wear and tear against the sharp edges of your skis/board and from rubbing against snow and ice. Consequently, they are reinforced in the crucial areas to withstand this, whereas a less resilient pair of trousers will soon rip. Proper skiing trousers also manage the technical achievement of not only being insulated to keep you warm against the winter weather and waterproof to keep you dry, but also breathable so you don't overheat – clever eh?

Make sure you try on the trousers before you buy, and ensure they are large enough to bend easily at the knees and the hips, without any restriction of movement. However much you like the look of them, if you can't bend down to do your boots up while wearing them, you'll feel like a bit of a plonker.

Thermals

You won't always need thermals, but for those days when the temperature drops, you'll be happy you packed them. Comfort and warmth are the main factors here. It's worth having thermal leggings to go under your ski trousers and a thermal short-sleeved or long-sleeved top to wear as a base layer beneath your regular clothing. This base layer will wick the sweat away from your body to stop you from getting cold.

These can be bought pretty much anywhere – from Marks & Spencer to more specialist sports stores.

'Never, ever think you can save the cost of buying ski trousers by wearing your old denim jeans! It has to be one of the most miserable items of clothing to wear when wet and cold.'

Gloves

These are a must. Wool gloves will not provide the insulation you need and will get wet through pretty quickly, so always go for insulated, waterproof gloves. Many skiing-specific gloves also have reinforced areas providing extra protection against the sharp edges of your skis or snowboard.

Some people prefer mittens to gloves, and find they help to keep their hands warmer.

A top tip for people who suffer from cold hands is to invest in some hand warmers – these are little pouches that slip into your glove or mitten and emit heat when activated. You can also get these to go in your shoes. They're on sale in most outdoor stores in both the UK and in resort.

'Wool gloves will not provide the insulation you need and will get wet through pretty quickly, so always go for insulated, waterproof gloves.'

Hat

You lose a lot of body heat through your head, so a hat is an absolute must. Whatever warm hat suits your style – from beanie to Russian Cossack – it's fair game on the mountain. However, it is worth having a hat that covers your ears, providing extra warmth.

Eyewear

Having correct eye protection is a serious matter. The snow reflects the sunlight up into your face, increasing its intensity and the impact it has on your eyes. People have suffered from snow blindness due to being in snowy mountains without adequate eye protection. The two main types of eyewear worn in the winter mountains are goggles and sunglasses.

Goggles provide the best protection against snow and cold and are essential in snowy weather. They are also very secure, so many people choose to wear them regardless of the weather. They do, however, tend to cover half your face, leaving you with rather strange suntan marks by the end of your trip. For this reason, some people prefer to wear sunglasses.

When shopping for goggles, it's worth buying a well-ventilated pair with double-lenses, as they should not mist up as readily as the single-lensed variety.

Many goggles come with interchangeable lenses that are designed for use in a variety of weather conditions:

- Black/polarised lenses reduce glare and are suitable for those bright, sunny days that we all dream about.

- Green/silver lenses are suitable for most bright weather conditions.

- Yellow/amber/gold lenses are suitable for most conditions, but especially low to moderate light.

- Purple/rose lenses are best in low-light conditions (flat light).

- Clear lenses are best for dark conditions, such as sunset or cloudy conditions.

If you choose to wear glasses, make sure they protect against UV rays, are securely attached and not prone to bouncing off your face if you go over a bump. It's also worthwhile picking a style that wrap nicely around your face and don't allow large amounts of direct sun in round the sides.

Remember: when you're out in the snow, the sun is not only coming at you from above, but also bouncing back at you off the snow.

Socks

Thick socks, thin socks, one pair, two pairs – everyone has their personal preference and only trial and error will help you find the right combination for you and the boots you're wearing. However, a good starting point is a long, thick pair of walking socks. These will keep your feet warm and also provide a bit of extra padding.

The main point to think about here is that you don't want a pair of socks where all the elastic has gone, so they slowly fall down and ruck up beneath the arch of your foot – this can be intensely annoying.

I personally prefer a knee length pair so that the boot does not rub directly on my skin.

Specific ski socks will have extra padding in the main pressure spots – at the heel and the front of the feet, helping to reduce discomfort.

Protection

Helmets

In most resorts, there are no rules on whether you should wear a helmet or not – it is at your discretion. However, it only takes a relatively minor bump to the head to cause potentially serious damage.

I would advise that you do wear a helmet at all times, as it's not a risk worth taking. If you are spending a lot of time in the snow park, or off piste where there could be hidden rocks buried unseen in seemingly safe powder, then it is even more imperative that you invest in one.

Ski helmets are sold in all ski equipment stores and come in a variety of sizes and styles. Make sure you buy one that is comfy to wear, as you're going to be even less likely to wear it if it's uncomfortable.

Wrist guards

You can buy gloves with built-in wrist guards, or separate strap on wrist guards that fit under your gloves. These are not essential – it's down to personal choice whether you wish to wear them or not.

Back protectors

In a similar vein to the strap on wrist guards, you can buy flexible protectors for the back, bum and shoulders – sometimes referred to as body armour – that are strapped on next to the body, beneath the clothing. Wearing these is once again down to personal choice.

Summing Up

- It's possible to hire clothing, so if this is your first trip and you're not sure whether you're going to like it or not, then this could be the right option for you.

- When buying a jacket, check it has a snow skirt.

- Gloves and hats are a must – ensure they are comfortable and fit well. Gloves must not be made of wool – ensure they are insulated and waterproof.

- Wear glasses that protect against UV rays.

- Helmets are not compulsory – but it's advisable to wear one.

Chapter Four

Location, Location, Location

When to go

In the northern hemisphere (Europe, US, Canada, Japan), the main winter season is from mid-December to mid-April. In the southern hemisphere (New Zealand, Australia), the main season is from May to October.

Although the opening dates for the resorts are set in advance, and tour operators will be booking guests up to a year in advance, there's no controlling when it will actually start snowing. Sometimes the snow comes later than usual, sometimes earlier. Sometimes the end of the season sees fresh snowfall and the lifts stay open until May, and sometimes you can see green grass at the start of April. For this reason, it's always safer to book your holiday for some time in the middle of the season, rather than risk either end.

Where to go

If you're based in the UK, the most easily accessible winter sport destinations are in Europe and then the US and Canada. New Zealand, Australia and Japan also have some great skiing, but they're a lot further to travel to!

If visiting Europe, the main ski resorts are found in France, Austria, Switzerland, Andorra, Italy, Scandinavia, Bulgaria, Spain – the list goes on. There are a number of different ways to get to these countries, including by car, by train and by plane, providing you with an element of control over timings and cost.

'Although the opening dates for the resorts are set in advance, and tour operators will be booking guests up to a year in advance, there's no controlling when it will actually start snowing.'

However, once in resort, the cost of living can be high, with a beer and plate of chips at a mountain restaurant requiring you to take out a second mortgage on your house!

If heading out to North America, you are obviously forced to make a long flight, with a significant difference in time zone. This is an expensive initial outlay, but a lot of the day-to-day amenities are more reasonably priced once you are out there.

New Zealand, Australia and Japan are in a league of their own, and apologies in advance for pointing out the obvious, but that's one hell of a transfer you've got in order to get there! Not so well-suited to the traditional week long skiing holiday. Although great destinations, they don't offer anything better than North America or Europe. Due to the extra time and cost involved in travel, I would suggest that you don't put these at the top of your ski holiday destination list, unless planning on extending your trip and exploring the country further. However, this is only my personal opinion – your destination is your choice!

'France offers a huge ski area. The majority of resorts are situated in the beautiful French Alps mountain range, on the Swiss and Italian border, with its deep valleys and dramatic rocky peaks and ridges.'

Resorts

How do you decide which resort to go to? There are so many options – where should you start? The question to ask yourself is what are your requirements? What are you looking to get out of your holiday? Are you going away with the kids, or do you want to party? Do you want somewhere picturesque, or are having the amenities on your doorstep more important?

France

France offers a huge ski area. The majority of resorts are situated in the beautiful French Alps mountain range, on the Swiss and Italian border, with its deep valleys and dramatic rocky peaks and ridges. There is also a scattering of resorts found in the French side of the Pyrenees and the Andorran border.

There are more than 200 ski resorts in France offering an enormous variety of destination. Everyone is catered for: from the serious off-piste explorer to beginners, from party animals to family groups.

The large number of resorts means that all accommodation options are catered for. However, resorts can get very busy during school holidays and are more expensive than many other countries.

Some of the lower ski resorts have developed from existing alpine villages, but a number of the higher ones have been designed and built with one thing in mind – ski holidays! They are not always the most picturesque of destinations, but this is often offset by amazing views and the pleasure of being able to ski right to the front door of your accommodation. Many holiday makers choose to forsake the picturesque resorts in favour of the better snow conditions that some of these purpose built, higher altitude resorts offer.

One of the best things about France is that it's home to some of the largest linked ski territories, including the famous Trois Vallees (comprising of Meribel and Mottaret, Val Thorens and Courchevel) and the newly linked 'Paradiski' area (Les Arcs and Les Plagne). These are areas where interlinking lift systems connect a number of different resorts, providing skiers and snowboarders access to miles of pistes and some of the longest ski runs in the world.

French resorts tend to have well-maintained pistes and increasingly modern lift systems. A number of them sport their very own glacier, meaning they have guaranteed snow. They range from the highest resort in Europe – Val Thorens – to some much lower resorts, for example Megeve. Although beautiful, some of the lower resorts do have sometimes unreliable snow conditions, especially in the increasingly erratic weather conditions that have been experienced recently. However, French resorts tend to have very good snow making facilities, in the form of snow cannons that provide snow cover on the lower slopes if required.

French resorts have a comparatively relaxed attitude when it comes to exploring the mountain, excellent ski schools and, of course, great food!

'The Swiss Alps are stunningly beautiful and contain a diverse collection of world-class ski resorts,'

Switzerland

Switzerland conjures up images of picturesque mountains, the *Sound of Music*, and Heidi skipping across rolling hills. All clichés out the window, the Swiss Alps are stunningly beautiful and contain a diverse collection of world-class ski resorts, offering a more traditional alpine experience than many of the French resorts.

Switzerland is famed for its efficiency, and this is never more obvious than in its public transport systems, providing easy accessibility to its resorts. This high level of service also spills over into its accommodation and eateries.

Home to more mountains over 4000m than any other European country, Switzerland houses some iconic peaks – and names such as the Eiger and the Matterhorn evoke images of hardened mountaineers and infamous expeditions.

Swiss ski resorts tend be very attractive and provide a good variety of accommodation. However, some resorts are very expensive, for example Klosters. Despite this, a resort to suit every need can be found in Switzerland.

Austria

Another world-class ski destination, Austria is home to some truly beautiful alpine ski villages. This is a very friendly country, with good accommodation and hearty food – although not recommended for vegetarians, unless a pure cheese diet sounds good to you!

Austria's resorts are generally smaller than their larger Swiss and French cousins, and even the larger resorts are often just a series of connected villages. This can work to the advantage of those on a budget, as the villages tend to be cheaper yet provide access to a larger linked ski area.

Resorts do tend to be at a lower altitude, and although they provide lift links up to high ski areas and glaciers, the villages themselves are often below the snow line. It's up to you to decide which is more important to you: beautiful alpine villages and great fun après-ski, or large ski areas with on-piste accommodation.

Andorra and Spain

This is a lesser known area for skiing. Plenty of sunshine, friendly locals, great food and great night life, but at a much cheaper price than the more northerly European ski resorts. Resorts in Andorra and Spain are a great place for ski holidays on a budget.

Check the snow forecast before you book your trip though, as the sunny weather can make snow conditions a bit hit and miss. These resorts tend not to be so good for snow parks either.

Bulgaria and Slovenia

Situated in the east of Europe, the main draw of Bulgarian ski resorts is that they offer some of the cheapest ski packages available. For this reason, there are a lot of UK visitors to these resorts taking advantage of the cheap and cheerful ski deals. If you're after a bargain, and a serious party, it's hard to beat.

Slovenia has a thriving ski scene and is an easy country to travel around, boasting some very attractive resorts that have not been quite so over run by UK tourists. Good quality accommodation can be found here, still at affordable prices, but resorts tend to be a lot smaller.

Both countries have less expert ski terrain and are better suited to a beginner or intermediate skier or snowboarder.

Germany

Although not yet a major ski destination for the Brits, the German Alps, otherwise known as the Bavarian Alps, are becoming more and more popular every year. They offer a large selection of predominantly quiet resorts with good snow and modern lifts.

Italy

Italy is the home of good value ski holidays that are perfect for families. With resorts spread between the Italian Alps and the dramatically beautiful Dolomites, there is a large selection on offer, and the great food is the icing on the cake. However, the Dolomites can get warm later on in the season, and the lift systems can be a bit dated. Nevertheless, the stunning views more than make up for it.

'Slovenia has a thriving ski scene and is an easy country to travel around, boasting some very attractive resorts that have not been quite so over run by UK tourists.'

Scotland

With a handful of resorts to choose from scattered across the Highlands, it would be rude to ignore Scotland's offering to the world of skiing, right on our doorstep. In fact, if you're unsure whether skiing and snowboarding are for you and are concerned about the cost involved in organising an overseas holiday, a couple of days in Scotland could be a great introduction to the sport without breaking the bank.

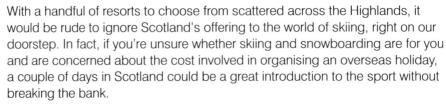

Scotland's resorts don't have the same high altitude as Alpine resorts, so best not to risk booking too early or late in the season.

Canada

'A couple of days in Scotland could be a great introduction to the sport without breaking the bank.'

Although Canada is a more expensive destination, and less convenient to get to than many of the European resorts, once tried, never forgotten! Canadian resorts have managed to combine the best of US and European resort styles, with friendly locals and phenomenal skiing!

The average winter temperature is a lot colder than in Europe, meaning better snow conditions and wonderful light fluffy powder! The authorities are not as strict as their American cousins when it comes to going off piste, although it's still far more restrictive than in Europe. However, the organised pistes, lift systems and beginner areas mean Canadian resorts are great for families and novices.

Despite all this though, Canadian resorts don't provide the same long, deep valleys and dramatic, rocky peaks and ridges as the European Alps, but the fantastic snow more than makes up for it.

USA

America provides an enormous variety of winter resorts catering for every taste and skiing level, and with a few Stetson-wearing cowboys thrown in for good luck.

The Americans are world experts at customer service and efficiency, and you'll be wrapped in cotton wool and swept along through your day in a soft comfortable cloud of 'please', 'thank you' and 'have a nice day'.

The efficiency and organisation of the resorts and lifts is second to none – however, it is not a cheap option. Not just because of the long flight and transfer times, but the in-resort costs are much higher than in Europe.

Off the beaten track

For those of you who like to go a bit left-field when choosing a travel destination, there are some slightly more unusual locations to head to, including Morocco, Iran and India.

The five best...

Resorts for off-piste aficionados

Choose a resort with high snow fall, low temperatures and extensive un-pisted areas. Also look out for recommended off-piste trails.

- Chamonix, France.
- La Grave, France.
- Engelberg, Switzerland.
- St Anton, Austria.
- Whistler, Canada

Resorts for beginners

Useful features include lots of easily accessible nursery slopes, a good ski school and accommodation near the slopes.

- Killington, US.
- Lech, Austria.

'For those of you who like to go a bit left-field when choosing a travel destination, there are some slightly more unusual locations to head to, including Morocco, Iran and India.'

- Peisey Vallandry, France.
- Jasper, Canada.
- La Plagne, France.

Resorts for nightlife

Look out for great après-ski bars and live music.

- Val d'Isere, France.
- Whistler, Canada.
- Breckenridge, US.
- Mayrhofen, Austria.
- Pas de la Casa – Grandvalira, Andorra.

Resorts for freestyle

Choose a resort with an extensive snow park, ideally not at resort level in case snow fall is poor or arrives late.

- Les Deux Alpes, France.
- Whistler, Canada.
- Les Arcs, France.
- Breckenridge, US.
- Snow Park, New Zealand.

Picturesque resorts

Choose a resort that has grown up around an old village, rather than a purpose built resort. Avoid the big high-altitude French resorts, as these tend to be dominated by ugly concrete apartment blocks.

- Megeve, France.

- Courmayeur, Italy.

- Grindelwald, Switzerland.

- Alpbach, Austria.

- Wengen, Switzerland.

Resorts for emptying your wallet

Look out for people wearing designer clothing and members of the royal family.

- Megeve, France.

- Courchevel, France.

- Klosters, Switzerland.

- Aspen, US.

- Verbier, Switzerland.

For further information on which resort to visit and for up-to-date reports on weather and snow conditions, check out the Ski Club of Great Britain's website at www.skiclub.co.uk.

Summing Up

- Think about what you want from your ski holiday before you choose which resort to go to.

- Bear in mind what level skier or snowboarder you are – some resorts have more advanced terrain than others.

- Where possible, avoid booking a trip at the very beginning or very end of the season, as snow coverage is less predictable.

Chapter Five

Planning Your Trip

You've just made the best decision of your life – you're going to go on your first winter snow holiday. You know when to go and where to go, you've made a list of what you need to pack, you've swatted up on skiing and snowboarding, and you even know the name of the guy who first invented snowboards for goodness sake. But how do you actually go about organising the holiday?

Package ski holidays

If planning your very first ski holiday, you could do a lot worse than booking a package. There's no denying that there's a lot to organise on a ski trip – from transport and accommodation, to lift passes and equipment hire. This can be a bit baffling for a first timer, and the beauty of a package ski holiday is that all this is organised for you!

There are more tour operators than I have space to mention here, but for a selection of the most reputable ones have a look at the help list.

I would advise that you think carefully about which operator you go with – some cater more to families, some are better with young crowds and others specialise in off piste or snowboarding. As with all things, there's a range of quality offered – from cheap apartments to luxury catered chalets.

A package holiday will not only arrange your international transport, but it will also arrange the transfer from the airport to your accommodation. They will organise your accommodation for you and, if you so desire, a rep will organise your ski pass, equipment hire and ski lessons. For a first trip out, you can't go wrong really.

'If planning your very first ski holiday, you could do a lot worse than booking a package.'

Also, for those watching the pennies, if you're not too fussed on destination or quality of your accommodation, you can book last minute deals at really reasonable prices.

Other services offered by most ski tour operators include a nanny/crèche service – although some resorts/accommodation options are better geared up for childcare than others, and operators will be able to advise you accordingly. Resort reps also organise quiz nights, bar crawls, meal nights, tobogganing and a whole host of other entertainment options if you're up for it. Be warned: they do earn commission on selling all these extras, so brace yourself to say no if it's not your scene!

The downside of going on a package ski holiday is that your fate is in their hands – if you're unlucky enough to find yourself with an incompetent rep or resort team, the old adage of 'if you want something done properly then do it yourself' can ring very true.

'The benefit of organising your own ski holiday is that you have control over all the different elements, rather than having to fit in with someone else's schedule.'

Independent ski holidays

The benefit of organising your own ski holiday is that you have control over all the different elements, rather than having to fit in with someone else's schedule. The downside is that you have control over all the different elements – and there can be a lot to organise. But don't let this put you off – you'll soon work out what needs doing. In the meantime, we have put together a handy breakdown of what needs to be arranged.

Accommodation

The first thing you need to decide on is your budget. This will help steer you through what type of accommodation you can realistically book. The main accommodation options are:

- Self catering apartment – this is probably the cheapest way to have a ski holiday. It can be loads of fun, giving you complete freedom to do what you want, when you want. On the downside, the apartments can be tiny, often telling you they sleep a certain number of people, only for you to realise on arrival that the sofas are counted as beds and there are bunks set up in the hallway.

- Hotel – the benefit of hotel accommodation is having all the facilities in one place, including restaurant, bar and often games room and spa facilities. On the downside, there are fixed meal times and nowhere private, other than your bedroom, to relax.

- Catered chalet – a catered chalet is basically a private ski lodge staffed by one or two 'hosts' who will cook you breakfast and dinner – they'll even make you a packed lunch if you ask nicely – and keep your rooms and the rest of the property nice and clean throughout the week. These come in a variety of different sizes – from small and intimate to a large chalet/hotel, but all have a relaxed atmosphere and provide good old fashioned home cooking. On the downside, if you're staying in a larger chalet, unless a big group of you have booked the whole thing out, you may well be sharing your dinner table with a number of other parties. However, this added sociability could come under the pros list for some people.

Transport

This very much depends on where you're going. If going to Europe, there are a number of options.

- Self drive – if you have the time then driving can be a fun addition to your holiday. This is best suited to holidays in the French Alps, as you can get there from Calais in a day, and the drive takes you through some beautiful French countryside. The further away your destination though, the less of a realistic option this becomes.

- Coach – various companies offer coach transfers from the UK out to resort. This enables you to enjoy the countryside while sitting back with your feet up. Although, you do have to travel according to their timetable.

- Train – the Eurostar takes you quickly and comfortably from our shores to Lille or Paris. You can then hop on one of the even more wonderful French

TGV trains, which will whisk you away to the nearest station to your resort. You will then have to hire a car, get a taxi or, depending on the resort, hop on a resort transfer bus to get up to your final destination.

- Ski train – this is a train service that travels between London and the French Alps every Friday night during the winter months. The train service is geared up for ski holiday makers and has lots of luggage storage space for not only suitcases but also those awkwardly shaped skis and snowboards. The ski train is especially great for those of you who want to get the party started a bit earlier, as it has a dedicated party carriage, equipped with licensed bar and filled with fellow revellers with no intention of sleeping.

- Flying – during the winter, most international airports in the UK will offer flights to the main entry ports for the ski fields across the world. Depending on your budget, you have the choice between both budget air carriers and the not so budget ones! A lot of the main resorts will have bus routes running regularly between the airports and resort. If you're going to one of the few resorts that don't have this then it's worth Googling airport transfers for your chosen resort, as there are often private companies that you can pre-arrange to pick you up at your arrival time. If there are a few of you then hiring a car at the airport can prove cost effective – if staying self-catered, the extra bonus of this is you can stop and do a big food shop in the valley, rather than in resort where everything costs twice as much.

Lessons

Lessons are available from in-resort ski schools for adults and children, novices and experts, skiers and snowboarders alike. They can be lots of fun and I would say essential if you've never skied/boarded before. Lessons will benefit you for the rest of your skiing years. You'll get so much more pleasure from being able to ski or snowboard properly than through trying to teach yourself and most likely picking up bad habits in the early days, which, like all bad habits, are a lot harder to lose than they are to pick up. Lessons are also a great way to instil confidence, and even once past the stage of being a beginner, the odd lesson every now and then can be really beneficial.

'Lessons will benefit you for the rest of your skiing years. You'll get so much more pleasure from being able to ski or snowboard properly than through trying to teach yourself.'

There tends to be more of an ethos in snowboarding than in skiing to not bother with lessons and instead try and teach yourself. This does work for some people – especially if competent in other board sports such as skateboarding – but even if you can only afford one or two lessons, it's money well spent.

Most resorts will have a number of different companies offering lessons for both children and adults. Resorts tend to have quite strict regulations of who can operate as a ski lesson provider, so as long as you book through a proper company rather than through someone advertising as an individual, you'll be fine. If you're going during a busy time of the season (busy times being Christmas/New Year, February half term and the school Easter holidays) then it's definitely worth booking lessons in advance as they get booked up very quickly. In fact, I'd advise you do this whatever date you plan to go, just to be on the safe side. Just go to the resort website where you'll find contact details for the resort ski schools. Most resort websites have the option to translate into English if necessary, so look for the UK flag or the 'English' button at the top of the page.

In general, lessons are offered as either a full day (with a break for lunch, where you can go back to your accommodation if you wish to) or a half day in either the morning or afternoon. Depending on your budget, you can either book onto a group or a private lesson. Joining in with a group lesson is the more economical way to do it, but you may have to commit to a full week. If opting for private lessons, there is more flexibility in what you choose to do – from just a single hour one morning, to the full works.

If you're a complete novice, and budget allows, I would recommend you have a week of half-day lessons. This gives you time to practise what you've learnt in the other half of the day and go out and have some fun on your own – it is a holiday after all! If you plan on partying every night, or are just not good in the mornings, then I would book your lesson for the afternoons, as morning ski school tends to start around 9am to 9.30am.

Likewise, if booking your children into lessons and heading off on your own, think about how the lesson timings fit in with your own plans. If you book them into a full day, you still have to come and collect them for the lunch time break, although for an extra cost many ski schools offer a lunch time supervision service.

Half-day lessons tend to run for 2-3 hours, starting at around 9am in the morning and 2pm in the afternoons, with a break for lunch. The instructor will meet you, or your child, at a pre-arranged meeting point in resort – usually near the base of the main lift up out of resort. They will then accompany the class through the whole lesson, bringing you all safely back to the same spot at the end of the lesson.

There are a few things to bear in mind when booking your lesson. If in a non-English speaking country, it's highly likely, unsurprisingly, that a lot of the instructors won't speak English. However, you'll be surprised at how much can be communicated through sign language, diagrams drawn in the snow and a few basic words. If you feel strongly about having an English-speaking instructor, make sure you ask for one. If that ski school doesn't have any, try another.

Secondly, if booking lessons for an adult, make sure you stress at the time of booking that you want to be in an adult's class. Adults and children are not taught in the same classes. There's nothing quite as bad for the self-confidence than being shown up by a group of eight year olds! However, if you do wish to learn together as a family then book a private lesson for you all to share.

When you book a lesson, make sure you find out where the meeting point is before you confirm. Some resorts are spilt into different levels, and you don't want to be expected to meet at 9am when your chalet is half an hour's ski away, particularly if you've never skied before!

For complete novices, lessons will take you through the following:

- Putting on your skis/snowboard.
- Using the ski lifts.
- Moving forward and learning the correct stance.
- How to stop.
- How to get down the slope safely and control your speed.
- Turning and edging.

More information on the above can be found in chapters 1 and 2. Skiing and snowboarding are two very different techniques, so classes are never mixed.

Everyone learns at different rates and the instructor will progress at a pace that's appropriate to the student.

Skiing with children

Many of the larger ski schools also offer a kindergarten service. This is a non-skiing childcare service for children out of nappies, from around age two. Kids' ski lessons are then usually available from age three to four. Some ski schools will also provide lunch and lunchtime supervision for an extra price, to enable parents to stay out and enjoy skiing all day.

Group snowboard lessons for children are not offered until the child is a little older – this age varies depending on the country and ski school, but it can be as old as 12 with some suppliers. This is because learning to snowboard can be very tiring, and very small children tend to be exhausted after an hour. Also, the position on skis tends to be a bit more intuitive for small children to pick up, compared to the sideways snowboard stance. Therefore, many children first learn to ski and then move onto snowboarding when they're a bit older. If you wish to book them a snowboarding lesson at a younger age, you'll need to book a private lesson.

The main advice when teaching children to ski is to keep it fun and easy. Make sure they are wearing appropriate clothing and don't get cold. Children have a higher surface area to volume ratio than adults and get cold a lot easier. Pop some energy boosting snacks in their pocket for when they get tired, and ensure they have plenty of breaks.

For small children, mittens are a better option than gloves. They're warmer and easier to get little hands into. It's worth attaching the two mittens by a long piece of string threaded through the sleeves of their jacket, or around each wrist. Otherwise, you risk spending all day hunting around beneath ski lifts for dropped gloves. Likewise, attach their lift pass to them securely.

If collecting your child from ski school at the end of the day, a nice idea is to take a sledge with you so you can give them a lift back – they're going to be tired, and the walk back from ski school to the accommodation, in ski boots and trying to carry skis, can be the straw that broke the camel's back!

In chapter 3 we discussed hiring clothing rather than buying it outright, for people who are unsure whether they want to commit to buying their own gear before they've tried skiing for the first time. Children's ski clothing can also be hired from a number of UK companies, including www.edge2edge.co.uk. In addition to clothing, children's helmets can be hired as well. With Edge2Edge, you have the option of having your hired clothing and equipment not only being delivered to your home, but also to select UK airports and even directly to some of the larger French resorts.

Equipment hire

If you don't already own your equipment, everything can easily be hired in resort. In fact, while you're still a beginner, it's advisable to hire equipment rather than buy your own – not just because it's expensive to buy and there's a chance (although it pains me to admit) that you might not want to come again, but also because you're more likely to scratch or damage your skis or board when you're learning.

There was a time when the equipment you got from hire companies was of a pretty poor standard, but these days hire shops have a really good selection of modern, good quality, technical skis, boards and bindings. They look after them well, ensuring the bases and edges of the skis and boards are kept in good condition, and the boots are kept clean and hygienic.

It's worth booking your equipment in advance though – all the major hire shops will have their contact details on the resort website – as during the busier periods they may not have enough stock. Even worse, they'll delve into their back catalogue of ancient battered skis and boards rather than turn a customer away!

It's worth letting the hire shop know what you want from your ski or board, and what level you're at. The better skier/snowboarder you are, the better ski/snowboard they'll give you.

'If you don't already own your equipment, everything can easily be hired in resort. In fact, while you're still a beginner, it's advisable to hire equipment rather than buy your own.'

If at the end of the first day your feet are in agony, then don't hesitate to go back to the hire shop and ask for a different sized boot.

Busy times

If you're not restricted to going away during school holidays, it's best to avoid them. The cost of accommodation and transport is pushed up during these times, and the resorts are a lot busier as well.

Don't forget...

- Sun cream – your winter skin won't know what's hit it when you get up above the clouds into beautiful sunshine, intensified by the snow. And on that note, some cooling aftersun lotion is also a must have.

- Muscle rub and ibuprofen – these can be a pleasant relief at the end of a particularly strenuous day.

- Comfy clothes for the evening and a pair of boots with good grips for walking around resort. Some soft shoes or slippers are also good for wearing around your accommodation, as you won't want to be traipsing snow and mud throughout the place. And don't forget your swimmers – even if your accommodation doesn't have its own pool, most resorts have a central pool (with sauna if you're lucky) which can be a wonderfully relaxing way to spend an afternoon off – especially if it's snowing.

- Some resorts still require a passport photo to go on your ski pass. To save the hassle of trying to find somewhere to do this in resort, have some taken at home and bring them out with you.

Ski pass

You should head to the lift pass office in your resort as soon as you can to buy your ski pass. The lift pass offices are usually located near the bottom of the main ski lift out of resort, and/or in the centre of the resort. This is one of the most expensive bits of the trip and unfortunately there are no cost-saving tricks

'You should head to the lift pass office in your resort as soon as you can to buy your ski pass. The lift pass offices are usually located near the bottom of the main ski lift out of resort, and/or in the centre of the resort.'

here – you can't be without one. When planning your trip, check on the resort website how much this will cost you and start saving then and there – you don't want to be stung by having this as an unexpected and unbudgeted cost when you arrive in resort. Before you get to the front of the queue, think about how many days you want to ski or board and what areas of the mountain you want to access. A lot of resorts have a central area, but then an upgraded pass will give you access to various satellite areas. However, if you're not going to be visiting these other areas and plan to stick to the main beginner slopes, then make sure you don't pay unnecessarily for the pleasure.

In resort services

The majority of resorts are well equipped with pharmacies, food shops, clothes stores, post offices, cash machines and even cinemas and swimming pools – but remember, although some resorts are purpose built, some are villages with residents who live there all year round.

However, you will find things cost a lot more in resort than down in the valley – this is because of the extra effort it takes to get supplies up there. If you're in self-catered accommodation and you have your own car, it's worth doing your food shop down in the valley. Not only will it be cheaper, but you'll also find a more extensive variety of products on offer.

Summing Up

- If you're going on a package holiday, read the small print carefully to find out what they will actually provide.

- If you require an English speaking ski instructor, make sure you ask specifically for one.

- Avoid booking over school holidays if you can.

- Always wear sun cream.

- Research the cost of a ski pass in the resort you're visiting and make sure it's included in your budget. Unfortunately, there are no cost-saving tricks for this.

- If you're in self-catered accommodation and have your own transport, do your food shopping down in the valley – it will be cheaper than in the resort.

Chapter Six
Preparation

Fitness first

A holiday skiing or snowboarding is one of the best things you'll ever do – but it's not the same as a week on a sun lounger. If you're serious about learning to ski or snowboard, remember it's a physical activity. It becomes easier as you get better, but even as an expert it's still serious exercise.

You'll find you get a lot more out of your trip, and consequently have a much more enjoyable time, if you get fit beforehand. As well as general cardio fitness that can be achieved through running or swimming, any exercise that builds on thigh and leg strength is well worth it.

A particular favourite is the 'squat and hold', where you press your back against a wall and squat down, as if you are sitting on a chair. Hold this position for 30 seconds, rest for 30 seconds, and repeat. As you get stronger, increase the time you hold the squat for.

Another good exercise is to stand on the edge of a step with just your toes, the rest of your feet hanging off the back. Then do 30 seconds of heel lifts, pushing up onto your toes and back down again. Rest, and repeat.

If nothing else, take the stairs rather than the lift on your way up to the office, and avoid the escalator when you go shopping. As the winter season approaches, you'll be surprised how many people join you!

When on your holiday, make sure you stretch your muscles in the morning before you head out – you wouldn't do other forms of exercise without some kind of warm up first, and the same applies here. By stretching out your muscles at the start of the day, you'll be less likely to pull something later on.

'If you're serious about learning to ski or snowboard, remember it's a physical activity. It becomes easier as you get better, but even as an expert it's still serious exercise.'

If you find your energy levels dropping during the day, pop an energy bar in your pocket, or some boiled sweets, to give you that extra boost when you need it. Or chill out with a cold beer on a sun terrace – you are on holiday after all!

Getting a head start

One great way to prepare for your first ever winter holiday is to have some lessons on an indoor 'real snow' slope in the UK.

You will get so much more pleasure from your holiday if you've got the initial learning stages under your belt before arriving in the mountains.

'One great way to prepare for your first ever winter holiday is to have some lessons on an indoor "real snow" slope in the UK.'

There are a number of these indoor real snow slopes scattered around the UK, and if possible I would advise going to one of these rather than a dry ski slope. A dry ski slope mimics the attributes of snow, but it is generally made from a brush-like, dry material. Although better than nothing, it doesn't prepare you quite as well as a real snow slope does.

The real snow slopes are great – they're in huge, cold, warehouse-sized rooms, where the temperature is regulated and the snow is just like the real thing. You need to wear proper ski clothing – and if you close your eyes, you can almost forget you're in a commercial estate in Milton Keynes!

The main centres in the UK are:

- SNO!zone Milton Keynes, Buckinghamshire.
- SNO!zone Castleford, West Yorkshire.
- SNO!zone Braehead, Glasgow.
- Tamworth SnowDome, Staffordshire.
- Chill Factore, Trafford Park, Manchester.
- The Snow Centre, Hemel Hempstead.

For full contact details, see the help list.

All these centres offer skiing and snowboarding lessons by qualified instructors. Equipment hire is thrown in as part of your entry fee, and for an extra cost you can borrow a jacket and trousers to wear while on the snow slope.

All the centres have fully equipped shops on site, where you can buy anything else you need – from ski gloves and hats, to boots and snowboards.

Piste categories

In resort, the maintained areas of the mountain (pistes) are clearly marked according to difficulty. Stay within the obvious markers as these indicate the edge of the piste. To help you plan your route, piste maps are displayed around resort and you can pick up a pocket-sized version when buying your lift pass.

The different piste categories in Europe, which are graded according to difficulty, are as follows:

- Green – indicates a flat, or nearly flat, piste. Easy beginner level. Often an access route.

- Blue – gentle gradient, beginner slope.

- Red – intermediate slope. Steeper and could be narrower than a blue slope.

- Black – advanced slope. Steeper, potentially narrow in places, or with a steep drop off at the edge. Not always maintained, so moguls (large bumps) can form.

In the US and Canada, they have a similar colour coding system. However, at the advanced end of the scale are 'black diamond' rated pistes, which are for advanced skiers/boarders, and 'double black diamond' rated areas, which indicate very advanced trails, often unpisted.

The beginner slopes will be clearly marked on the map, and are usually on the lower slopes.

'In resort, the maintained areas of the mountain (pistes) are clearly marked according to difficulty. Stay within the obvious markers as these indicate the edges of the piste.'

Ski lifts

One of the advantages of skiing and snowboarding is that you get to enjoy the excitement of going down, without the hard work of having to climb back up. There are a number of different types of ski lift that you'll encounter on the mountain, all of which can be used by anybody wearing skis or a snowboard.

- Chair lifts – these are metal chairs attached to a steel cable loop strung up between a series of pylons. Leave your skis or snowboard on and take a seat and allow yourself to be whisked up the mountainside. They have a safety barrier that pulls down over you, and most have a footrest for comfort. When getting on the chair lift, simply stand in the indicated area and let the chair, which will slow down but not stop, scoop you up from where you're waiting. At the top, raise the safety bar and slide off onto the exit piste. If on a snowboard, you will have to take your back foot out of its binding in order to propel yourself into the right position for getting on the chair – when the chair picks you up, and when you get off at the other end, just place your back foot on the board, next to your back binding, and allow the board to glide forwards.

- Cable cars – these are similar to chair lifts, but rather than a suspended chair on a steel cable, they consist of a suspended enclosed 'bubble', or carriage, on a steel cable. Take your skis/snowboard off to board the cable car and, depending on the size of the carriage, either carry them in with you or put them in the secure carrying cradles on the outside. Many cable cars have seats in them, providing a nice opportunity to have a breather, take off your gloves and hat, and relax, sheltered from the weather outside.

- Button lifts – these look like buttons on the end of a hanging pole, again suspended on a steel cable. Leave your skis/snowboard on for this lift. Slide up to the pole, taking the button between your legs. As the pole is pulled forward by the moving cable, the button between your legs will pull you along. The button will not support your weight, so don't try and sit down on it. At the top of the lift, simply release the button from between your legs and slide off onto the exit piste. If on a snowboard, these lifts are slightly more awkward due to the sideways stance adopted on a board. However, it all still works in the same way – just keep your board pointing in the direction you want to travel, and allow yourself to be pulled along.

'One of the advantages of downhill skiing and snowboarding is that you get to enjoy the excitement of going down, without the hard work of having to climb back up.'

- T-bar – these, fortunately, are not very common, and not very popular either. As with the button lift, you need to keep your skis and board on. The T-bar is like a button lift, but instead of a button it has a retractable upside down T hanging from it. Pull the upside down T towards you and rest one branch of the T underneath your buttocks. Then relax and allow it to pull you forwards. T-bars can either be ridden alone or a second skier can rest on the other branch of the T. You're both then pulled up together. When you get to the top, simply release the T-bar and glide off. If on a snowboard, don't panic – simply tuck one branch of the T underneath your front leg and allow it to pull you forward, releasing it when you get to the top. If on a snowboard, it's much easier not to double up on the lift with another rider.

Summing Up

- You will really benefit by exercising in preparation for a ski or snowboard holiday.

- Remember to always do some warm-up stretches at the start of a day's skiing or snowboarding.

- If preparing for your first ever trip, take some beginner ski or snowboard lessons at a real snow slope in the UK before you go – you won't regret it.

- Using a piste map, make sure you check the difficulty of a piste (green, blue, red, black) before committing to it.

- When on a chair lift, always pull the safety bar down.

Chapter Seven

Working a Ski Season

So, you've had your first taste of winter life and now you understand what all the fuss is about! You've experienced the beauty, felt the elation and realised just how addictive it is. What's that you say? You want more? Well dear reader, it sounds like you need to do a ski season…

The life of a seasonaire

There is no better way to improve your skiing or snowboarding than by working for six months out in a resort. And there's no greater pleasure than waking up every morning, looking out your window at snow covered mountains and knowing that this is home – well at least until the end of the winter.

If you're at a stage in life when you can afford the time, then I can't recommend doing a winter season highly enough.

There are a number of different ways to do a ski season. The first, and most enviable, is to have a massive bank account brimming over with funds – if that's the case then pick a resort, hop on the Internet and it won't take long to find an apartment up for rent for the season. Next step – head out to resort and be the most envied person around!

For those of you not lucky enough to have this option available, worry not – there are plenty of other ways you can fund yourself for a season.

'There is no better way to improve your skiing or snowboarding than by working for six months out in a resort.'

Am I too old?

There is no upper age limit on doing a season – yes, you have to have energy, and you have to be mobile and able to get around in what can be a seriously icy place, but other than that seasonal workers range from school leavers right through to retirement age.

I'm not going to lie to you, a lot of people who do seasons are of school/ university age, but don't let this put you off if you don't fall into this bracket – you'll be surprised what a varied group of people you find in resort, and how welcoming and accepting everyone is – remember, everyone in resort has one very big thing in common, a love of the mountains!

What job can I do?

The majority of jobs available are in the tourism industry. The big employers are the tour operators – see the help list for information on the major UK tour operators. The main jobs offered with them are listed below.

Hotels

The main jobs at hotels will be waiting and bar staff, chefs, kitchen staff, night porters, chambermaids, receptionists and managers/assistant managers.

Younger members of staff tend to take a lot of these hotel roles (management aside). Some hotels also employ masseuses or sports physios as part of their guest services. Be aware though – you may be expected to help out with the waiting staff/chambermaids during periods when you have no clients.

These jobs operate in shifts, so your working hours will vary throughout the season and will be set by your line manager. You will have one official day off a week and mornings and afternoons throughout the week to go out skiing or snowboarding.

Chalets

Being a chalet host involves cooking breakfast and dinner for your guests, sometimes making packed lunches, deep cleaning the property once a week when guests change over and surface cleaning the bedrooms and living areas every morning. Chalets are very intimate places, so unlike hotel work where you can get away in a lot of roles without integrating with the guests, working in a chalet will often require you to chat with the guests and really act as a host. Chalet jobs are often filled by a more mature seasonaire as you have to manage yourself on a daily basis, and a lot of chalets have live-in staff, so it really becomes home away from home. Plus, cooking a different, good quality meal every night requires experience.

The working hours of a chalet host are fairly set. You will be expected to provide breakfast each morning and then give the chalet a quick clean. Depending on the size of the chalet, this will normally take you from 7.30am to 10.30am – you then have the rest of the day to yourself! You then return to the chalet for afternoon tea and to prepare dinner at around 4.30pm/5pm. Once dinner is finished and you have cleared everything away, you have the rest of the evening to yourself. The only day different to this is transfer day, when the old guests leave and the new guests arrive – you'll be expected to strip and remake all the beds and deep clean the chalet. There is also chalet shop day, when you do your weekly shop – but with practice you'll be amazed how quickly you can get this done. You will have one official day off a week, where you lay out breakfast the night before – no cooked option that day – and guests go out to a restaurant for dinner.

Childcare

Most tour operators employ a team of qualified childcare professionals. These will either be assigned to a crèche in a specific hotel or a non-property specific resort crèche. This role will involve everything from daytime childcare and taking little ones to ski school, to babysitting duties in the evening. Once again, these jobs will work in shifts set by your line manager. You will have one official day off a week and will have mornings and afternoons throughout the week to ski or snowboard.

Resort rep

To be a resort rep you have to love interacting with guests, and having the gift of the gab always helps! You'll be expected to get up and talk in front of groups of guests, take them out on bar crawls and sell them lift passes and après-ski tickets (your monthly pay will be commission based, so a gift for sales is an advantage). You'll also be the key point of contact that customers complain to when things go wrong, as they invariably do, so a thick skin and good diplomacy skills are a bonus.

Your busiest day will be transfer day, when the old guests leave and the new ones arrive. Every coach load of new guests that arrives at the airport are met and accompanied back up to resort by a rep. You may go back and forth to the airport a number of times in one day. You will then conduct welcome talks for the new guests, letting them know all the services offered during their stay and trying to sell them as many extras as possible. During the week you will visit your allocated properties each day at a certain time, so if any guests have questions, they know when and where they can find you. You will also lead the après-ski events – whether it's a quiz night, bar crawl or night time tobogganing. You will have one official day off a week, and will be able to go up the mountain most days, as your daily duties don't usually start until the late afternoon property visits. You may be expected some days a week to take guests on a skiing/snowboarding tour of the pistes, or an away day to a local ski field.

Resort management

Each resort has a management team made up of, depending on the size of resort, a resort manager, assistant manager, accountant and chalet manager. They are responsible for staff welfare, in-resort budgeting, quality control and in-resort sales. As with the reps, transfer day will be your busiest time, managing the reps and dealing with any problems that arise with bookings and so on. During the week you manage your own working hours. You will have a mountain of paperwork that needs filling out and returning to head office each week, and will deal with any issues as and when they arise. In theory you have one official day off a week, but the truth is if a problem arises, you will be expected to deal with it. It's up to you to manage your working hours so that you get enough skiing time in. It's unusual for these management roles to go to someone who's never done a season before – it helps to have an understanding of how it all works in order to be able to do the job effectively.

Head office

Each tour operator will have an in-country head office. Jobs in these offices are full time and operate according to more regular office hours. They involve roles from finance and sales, to logistics and programme managers, and on average will pay more than the more domestic roles. These types of jobs are few and far between. You will work fixed hours, akin to office hours in the UK. Most roles will also be expected to work transfer days at the weekend – particularly if you are in logistics and manage the supply of transfers to and from airports and resorts, ensuring all guests get where they need to go, and all coach drivers turn up in the right sized coach at the right time…on the right day. Easier said than done! Realistically, you may only get a couple of days skiing a week, maximum.

Working in the USA or Canada

The main challenge to doing a season in North America is obtaining a working visa. Most UK tour operators' programmes are a lot smaller in the US and Canada than they are in Europe. Although they do employ UK staff to go and work out in the resorts, the number of visas they will provide are limited and often go to returning staff as a reward for loyalty. There are a number of other ways to obtain a working visa – depending on your age and situation, you can apply for one through BUNAC, but there are terms and conditions that have to be fulfilled in order to be eligible. See the help list for more information.

If you have managed to obtain a visa independently, a lot of ski areas in the USA and Canada hold job fairs in the autumn where you can go along and apply for work in a resort – from working in the mountain restaurants, to ski hire shops. In Europe, these jobs are usually taken by the locals and not really open to UK seasonal workers.

Working in New Zealand or Australia

If you're under 30, it's not too much of a problem to obtain a working visa for New Zealand or Australia, and BUNAC also provide visas if you fit their criteria.

When should I start applying for jobs?

Most tour operators start interviewing for jobs at the end of the previous winter, around spring. In general, job interviews will take place through the company's UK office. A great place to hunt for winter jobs, and where the majority of UK operators advertise, is www.natives.co.uk – everything you need on one site.

As previously mentioned, job fairs in the USA and Canada tend to take place in the autumn.

'It's great fun living with other staff members, as you get to know lots of people.'

Most tour operators will get all their staff out on training courses before the official start of the season – depending on your role, you will be expected to be available to go out mid-November/beginning of December. Most resorts have their first guests arriving in the middle of December.

Will accommodation be provided?

If you're working for a tour operator, accommodation will be provided. This can be very varied, depending on the size of resort and your job role: from your own private accommodation in the chalet where you're working, to a shared apartment with other staff or a shared chalet. It's great fun living with other staff members, as you get to know lots of people. However, if you have worries, reservations or special requirements, it's worth discussing these with your employer in advance of going out to resort, so preparations can be made. It's a lot harder to make changes once you're out there.

If you're a more mature applicant, it's also worth chatting with your employer well in advance of heading out to resort, as they will take your preferences into consideration where possible when allocating you to a resort and arranging accommodation.

If you've independently arranged your own work, accommodation may not be provided. However, there will be plenty of apartments in resort up for rent, but make sure you budget for it. Ask your employer to point you in the right direction, or a quick search on the Internet will soon find something.

Money makes the world go round…

…but not when working in a ski resort. You will not make your fortune doing a ski season. Unless you set up and run your own enterprise out there, you will not make even a fraction of your fortune. But don't let this deter you. If working for a tour operator, more often than not you'll be fed and watered, and once set up with equipment and lift passes, you'll be surprised at how little you want for. Doing a winter season is the perfect way to remind yourself that it's not what you earn that makes you happy.

Perks of the job

Most major employers will provide you with accommodation, lift pass and equipment hire as part of your employment package – but not all. If embarking on a season with no savings in your back pocket then it's vital you check, before applying for a job, what your employer will offer you in return. Equipment hire and lift passes are expensive, but essential.

Do I need any skiing experience?

In a word, no! People who have never seen snow before are just as welcome to work out in resort as those who have been skiing since birth. And there's no better way to learn than by doing it every day for six months. If you've never skied before though, don't apply for a job that requires you to guide guests on ski tours!

'People who have never seen snow before are just as welcome to work out in resort as those who have been skiing since birth. And there's no better way to learn than by doing it every day for six months.'

Buying your own equipment

So, you've got the bug. You've popped your winter cherry, you've fallen in love with the mountains and you're addicted. You know you're going to keep coming as often as possible, for as long as you're able, and the next obvious step is to buy your own equipment. Yes, it's a big investment, but it'll soon prove cost effective when you think of the money you would have spent on equipment hire.

Boots

Whether a skier or a snowboarder, the first items of equipment worth buying are a pair of boots – these are very personal to you as an individual. Hire boots often lose their shape on the inside due to having a variety of different shaped feet in them over the years. You won't believe the difference a pair of new boots makes, both in terms of comfort and performance.

In chapter 2, I mentioned that skiing and snowboarding boots are made up of an inner and an outer section. It's worth buying your boots from a store that is equipped to heat mould this inner part to fit the contours of your foot, increasing comfort and preventing those bony knobbly bits from rubbing. Some stores also offer customised insoles, which are moulded to precisely map the base of your foot, adding even more support and comfort.

A good sales assistant will ask you to take your shoes off, measure your feet and then analyse their shape – for example, do you have particularly wide or thin feet? Different brands are better suited to different foot shapes.

Let the sales assistant know what level of skier or snowboarder you are. Boots get stiffer as the standard of performance improves – they also get more expensive. Beginners' boots are softer, more forgiving, and in general more comfortable. More advanced skiers and boarders are sometimes willing to forgo comfort levels in order to gain a higher standard of performance.

Never buy a pair of boots online without trying them on first, no matter how appealing the price. You'll soon regret it after a morning of agony. The same goes with buying second-hand boots. If you're going to splash out and purchase a pair, then do it right and get a new pair.

'Whether a skier or a snowboarder, the first items of equipment worth buying are a pair of boots – these are very personal to you as an individual.'

Skis and snowboards

When out shopping for a new pair of skis or snowboard, a sales assistant who knows their stuff should ask you about what type of ski or snowboard you've previously been riding, and what sort of skiing or snowboarding you like doing – what gradients, speeds and grade of piste do you like to go on? Do you spend most of your time cruising with your family, or are you off hunting down untracked powder? Do you spend most of your time pulling tricks in the park?

As with all things, performance and price are linked. The sales adviser will be able to advise on length of ski or snowboard, based on your height, weight and the type of riding you prefer. And then, of course, there's the colour…

Looking after your equipment

The base

Keep an eye on the base of your skis or snowboard. If any deep scratches appear, take it to a ski technician, found in most equipment hire shops, as soon as possible – they will fill the scratch with a layer of 'p-tex' (a protective material used to repair skis and snowboards). It's very important to do this, as you don't want water to seep into the interior of your ski or board, causing it to lose its spring and flexibility.

It's also important to regularly wax the base, as this will stop it from drying out and will keep it running smoothly and freely over the snow. You will really notice the feeling if it needs waxing as the ski or snowboard will feel very 'sticky' when sliding over the snow – and you'll wonder why everyone is suddenly a lot faster than you!

At the end of the season, it's worth having the base waxed before you store your equipment away for the summer, as this will stop it drying out over the following months.

The edges

Both skis and boards have metal rims that run round the edge. It's important that the edges along the sides that have contact with the snow are kept nice and sharp, helping you to control the ski/board when turning and stopping, especially in icy conditions where you need extra control. Don't try to do this yourself, unless you have specialist equipment – ski technicians in most equipment hire shops will do this for you. You'll be able to feel when your edges need re-sharpening as the ski or board won't feel as responsive as normal and will feel as though it's skidding around.

Summing Up

- If you have the opportunity to do a full winter season, it's well worth taking.

- There are a wide range of different jobs out there, so do some research and try to pick one that you'll enjoy and that suits your personality.

- Before accepting your job offer, check whether your employer provides accommodation, a lift pass and equipment hire.

- If you decide to purchase your own equipment, make sure you buy from a ski or snowboard specialist, who will take your individual needs into consideration.

- Look after your equipment – wax your skis/snowboard regularly and make sure the edges are sharp.

Chapter Eight

Mountain Safety

Mountains are wonderful, spiritual places. Time spent there helps put all the worries of everyday life into perspective and reminds us of the beauty and wonder of the world around us.

But it should never be forgotten that mountains are serious places. Places that humans cannot control and cannot enforce rules on. With good road systems that get us deep into mountain ranges, and modern ski lifts that quickly whisk us away from the safety of the car park up into a world of high rocky peaks, sheer cliffs, powder bowls and adventure, it's very easy to find yourself all of a sudden in a wild place. All the piste markers and signposts in the world don't take away from the fact that mountains are potentially dangerous places that require respect.

This is not intended to instil fear in you – each year, thousands of people enjoy fun, safe holidays in the mountains – rather this is just a reminder that you're not in a controlled theme park.

If this is your first trip to the winter mountains, don't panic – the beginner pistes are often on the lower slopes, near the resort and easily accessible; a protected area for you to learn the basics and increase your confidence, before venturing higher up.

However, there is a certain 'green cross code' that is worth remembering when skiing or snowboarding, aimed at enhancing your safe enjoyment of the mountain, and the enjoyment of those around you.

'Mountains are wonderful, spiritual places. Time spent there helps put all the worries of everyday life into perspective and reminds us of the beauty and wonder of the world around us.'

On piste

'When heading down the piste, the person in front of you has right of way – remember, they don't have a rear view mirror so will not be aware of what you're up to. It's up to you to avoid them.'

- When heading down the piste, the person in front of you has right of way – remember, they don't have a rear view mirror so will not be aware of what you're up to. It's up to you to avoid them.

- It's very easy when concentrating hard to be unaware of what's going on around you – try to have a look around every now and then for where the edge of the piste is, any signposts or trees that you need to be aware of, whether there's a big change in gradient in the slope ahead, or a ski school standing in the middle of the piste.

- If entering another piste, check the way is clear before continuing so you avoid moving out into an oncoming skier's path.

- Expect the unexpected – if coming up behind someone, or overtaking someone, be prepared for them to potentially stop, turn, fall, or sprout wings and fly away, at any given moment. Slow down to try and synchronise your movements with theirs to avoid colliding head on.

- If crossing in front of another skier, avoid crossing too closely – if they fall, you don't want them taking you with them.

- When stopping, try to stop at the edge of the piste rather than over the brow of a hill or where oncoming traffic can't see you. Also, avoid stopping in a bottle neck or in the middle of a narrow path, therefore blocking the way for everyone else. These pointers all sound like common sense, but you'd be amazed how many people stop to take a photo just around a blind corner in the middle of the piste – and you'll be amazed how colourful your language can get when this happens!

- Always take note of piste signs – they're there for a reason. Not only will they send you in the right direction, but they'll also alert you if a piste is closed or if there is a hazard ahead.

- Make sure you know what time the lifts shut and how long it will take you to get back to resort. I've made this mistake before and been stuck in a valley having to sheepishly call my friends to make the long drive to collect me!

- If the weather closes in and you find yourself lost, then make sure you stick to the piste – piste markers line the boundaries of every piste and these can be followed if the visibility gets bad. Alternatively, lift stations and restaurants will be staffed, so don't hesitate to ask for help – worst-case scenario, you can always wait and go down with them at the end of the day. The most important thing is not to go off on your own – it can be very disorientating if a cloud and snow bank comes in, giving zero visibility.

- And finally, never throw your skis or board, no matter how frustrated you're getting. You'll be surprised how quickly they disappear off down the mountain, and how much speed they pick up!

Off piste

Part of the beauty and appeal of skiing off piste is that you're away from the crowds and off the beaten track. The thrill of being the first person to make tracks down a pristine snow field, with no sound but your own breathing, is what it's all about for me.

Now not all off piste is as off the beaten track as my little fantasy above – you could just as easily be riding down unpisted areas beneath a chair lift, or on the side of a piste. But when you go off piste, you are taking responsibility for your own safety and wellbeing. And the further off piste you delve, the more so this becomes.

Don't expect there to be signposts pointing you in the right direction, or warning signs when there's a cliff approaching – so tread carefully. If possible, it's always worth checking the route you want to take from a different angle so you can pin point any hazards that you may not be able to see from the top. And don't rely on following other unknown skiers or their tracks – they may not know where they're going either.

There are a few safety rules when off piste to minimise the risk to you and others:

- Avoid traversing sharply across the top of a powder slope, especially if there are skiers/boarders beneath you, as this could set off a slab avalanche.

- Always take into account the snow conditions – has there been recent heavy snowfall? Has it been very warm and then very cold? See the section about avalanches and safety equipment later in this chapter for more information.

'Part of the beauty and appeal of skiing off piste is that you're away from the crowds and off the beaten track.'

- Does the snow look like it has previously avalanched – are there broken lumps of snow and ice strewn across the area? If in doubt, don't go there.

- Beware of cornices. Cornices are lips of snow on the edge of a ridge that hang out over the drop. They're caused by the wind and if you walk or ski on top of them thinking they're solid, you run the risk of falling through.

Lifts

There are some general rules regarding ski lifts:

- Don't queue jump – lift queuing, although at times frustrating, is just part of the 'experience'. Often it's only the main connecting lifts out of resort that suffer from the larger queues, and sometimes there are no queues at all. With more and more fast modern lifts being installed, queues tend to move pretty quickly.

- Try not to step on, or put your poles on, other people's skis or boards. You're likely to scratch them or worse.

- Be prepared for the fact that ski schools often have their own entrance to the lifts, by-passing most of the queue. The pupils in the class will then go one at a time, sharing the lift with everyone else, spreading out their numbers over a series of lifts.

- If carrying a rucksack, carry it on your front when getting on a chair lift, so it's not forcing you off from behind when you go to sit down.

- On chair lifts, always pull the protective bar down to provide you with some security. Many of them have a foot rest attached which will move into place when you pull the bar down – this will make the ride a lot more comfortable.

- On button lifts and T-bars, try not to weave around or 'slalom' on your way up. This will rut up the snow for lifts riders coming up behind you.

- If you fall off a button lift or T-bar – as we all do from time to time – try to move out of the way as quickly as possible so you don't get in the way of the person coming up behind you. Don't be scared of these lifts though – you'll get used to them pretty quickly.

- When you get off the lift at the end, move out of the 'landing zone' as quickly as possible so there's space for the next people coming in behind you.

Avalanches

Avalanches are when a mass of snow breaks free and travels, often at great speeds, down the mountainside. They come in all shapes and sizes, from loose powder to solid slabs of snow.

The most common cause of avalanche is heavy snowfall – as the fresh snow increases it becomes heavier and heavier until gravity takes over and the snow breaks away from the mountainside. Risk is increased if the new snow has fallen onto a weaker area of snow. Strong wind also increases the risk of avalanche.

Slab avalanches occur in heavier snow, when a solid slab separates from the mountainside and slides down in one piece. These are sometimes triggered by skiers/boarders traversing sharply across the top of a steep untracked snow slope, especially later in the season when temperatures are higher and the untracked snow tends to be heavier. Be aware of this when traversing off piste, especially if there are people, or a pisted area, beneath you.

After a heavy snowfall, you will often hear loud explosions around the mountains. This is due to the mountain security teams intentionally triggering avalanches in high risk areas – by doing this in a controlled fashion, with no one else around, they reduce the risk of an avalanche occurring unexpectedly when there are skiers in the area.

Most avalanches occur on predominantly treeless slopes – the trees act to bind the snow together, reducing the risk. In fact, resorts sometimes plant trees on steep hillsides above residential areas as a security measure.

Whatever the type of avalanche, there is one common factor: it will take the most direct route down or be funnelled into a gully. If you're unlucky enough to be in the path of an oncoming avalanche then try to move out of the way by cutting left or right.

If concerned about avalanche risk, check the warning flags/signs at mountain information points. These will make it very clear if there is a high avalanche risk. If you're still concerned, then don't venture off piste that day. Never go off piste alone.

'After a heavy snowfall, you will often hear loud explosions around the mountains. This is due to the mountain security teams intentionally triggering avalanches in high risk areas.'

If you do need to get hold of the mountain rescue, then go to a member of staff working at the lift stations or in the restaurants and they will call them in for you. There is no emergency number for the mountain rescue which is why individuals should never go off piste on their own.

Safety equipment

Avalanche transceivers

If planning on spending a lot of time off piste, it's worth you and your party investing in avalanche transceivers. This is a small device that straps to your body beneath your jacket so it won't be pulled off.

The transceiver has two settings: one where it emits an electrical signal and one where it can detect the signal. Therefore, if one of your party is buried in an avalanche, your transceiver will detect them and provide you with directions to follow, helping you to locate them as quickly as possible. Likewise, if you're unlucky enough to be buried, your party will be able to detect and locate you.

All of your party need to be wearing a transceiver for this to be worthwhile. Always have it set to emit a signal, unless you're actively searching for someone – if caught in an avalanche, you won't have time to change the settings. It's essential all your team practise using the transceivers before taking them up the mountain, as there is a skill to following the signal and finding the buried transceiver. Get your friends to hide a transceiver in your back garden, for example, and practise locating it before taking it up the mountain. If the situation arises when you do have to use it in an emergency up on the mountain, you don't want to waste time trying to work out how it functions.

RECCO reflectors

Many jackets and trousers designed for use in the mountains come with a built-in RECCO reflector. The reflector requires no interaction by the wearer, but if it were to be buried in an avalanche it would be detected by a RECCO detector, which many, although not all, mountain rescue teams use.

Although definitely a good idea, in my opinion these are not a substitute for avalanche transceivers, as valuable search and rescue time is wasted waiting for the mountain rescue to arrive.

Avalanche probes

Probes are a crucial part of an avalanche rescue set-up, significantly speeding up the search process.

They are used to mark the exact location of the buried body. The transceiver will lead you to the spot where there's the least distance between you and the victim. But digging 50cm in the wrong direction can cause you to completely miss the body. This is where the probe comes in use, to pin point the exact spot.

Always stick the probe in at a 90° angle to the snow. A careful approach to the search is required here. Some people advise probing in ever increasing circles, around the point the transceiver has lead you to, each probe 50cm apart. Another technique is to follow a linear grid pattern. Whichever approach you choose, approach it methodically and stick to it.

When the body is located, you will feel a definite change in pressure when you try and push the pole down. Leave the probe in the snow as a marker.

Many probes have depth markers on them, giving you an indication of how deep you have to dig, and many fold away in the same way as tent poles, making them easy to pack in your rucksack.

The points to look for when purchasing an avalanche probe are:

- Length – make sure the probe is over 200cm long.

- Ensure the probe is quick and easy to assemble. Every second counts when searching for an avalanche victim.

- Choose a probe that is strong and unbreakable – ideally made from either carbon or aluminium, although the carbon probes are lighter. The mountain rescue professionals often use steel probes, as these are more durable when used frequently. However, they are a lot heavier to carry.

Snow shovel

Having an appropriate shovel, and knowing how to use it, is another essential part of avalanche rescue – there's no point locating the body if you can't then dig it out. Avalanche debris (the broken up snow left by an avalanche) can be very hard packed, and digging through it can be tough, making a strong shovel essential. However, this strength needs to be partnered with being light and compact, as you need to be able to carry the shovel easily in your rucksack.

Many shovels have telescoping handles, which extend when needed. It is also possible to find shovels where you can conveniently store the probe inside the hollow handle.

As with all avalanche equipment, it's important to practise using it in a safe environment before running the risk of having to use it in an emergency.

When the body has been located using transceiver and probe, rather than digging straight down around the probe, it is advisable to take a step back and dig in from the side. This means you are not potentially standing on the victim, blocking any airways or compressing the snow further onto them. Also, it is easier to remove the snow if digging in from the side rather than straight down.

Avalanche equipment manufacturers

The main manufacturers of avalanche transceivers, probes and shovels are:

- BCA – www.backcountryaccess.com.
- Black Diamond – www.blackdiamondequipment.com.
- Mummut – www.mammut.ch.
- Ortovox – http://en.ortovox.com.

Stores such as Snow+Rock and Ellis Brigham will stock the above equipment, as will mountain equipment shops in resort.

Altitude sickness

Ski resorts are by their very nature at a higher altitude than you're most likely used to. Not everyone is affected by altitude, but you may find your sleep pattern is disturbed or you feel a little light headed for the first couple of days. Don't panic – your body will get used to it. Drink lots of water as it's easy to get dehydrated in the dry mountain air, and if you feel really rotten when you take the ski lifts to the very top of the mountain, go lower down in resort again and you'll soon feel better.

Snow parks

A lot of resorts have a snow park, which is an area dedicated to jumps, rails and halfpipes. This is not a safe place for beginners. However, when you feel ready, the jumps are often graded in difficulty in the same manner as pistes – green for small jumps, red for intermediate and black for the impressively, often terrifyingly, large.

Never stand in the landing zone of a jump and take it easy – start off small. As with all things, keep the knees bent and stay low so your knees can absorb the pressure of the landing.

'Ski resorts are by their very nature at a higher altitude than you're most likely used to. Not everyone is affected by altitude, but you may find your sleep pattern is disturbed or you feel a little light headed for the first couple of days.'

Summing Up

- Mountains can be dangerous places. Stay safe by following the advice given in this chapter and by paying close attention to local piste, weather and safety updates provided by the resort.

- Be aware of the weather and snow conditions when skiing or snowboarding off piste.

- Don't queue jump at ski lifts.

- Use your common sense and try to be aware of what is going on around you when skiing or snowboarding on piste.

- If you're going to do a lot of off-piste exploring, be aware of avalanche risks and make sure all of your group are wearing avalanche transceivers – and know how to use them.

Chapter Nine

Odds and Ends

Although this book has focused on downhill skiing (or Alpine skiing as it's sometimes called) and snowboarding, don't be led into thinking the mountains during winter are the domain of these disciplines alone – far from it, there are a whole host of other activities you can do if you so choose.

Cross-country skiing

Cross-country skiing is how skiing first began, and was originally a way of getting from A to B in flat, snowy countries before it became a recreational pastime. Today cross-country skiing is a wonderful way of getting away from the crowds and enjoying some beautiful scenery.

These skis are not designed for hurtling down the mountain at great speeds – they are more designed to efficiently move across terrain.

The equipment is different, with the skis being longer and thinner. Plus the bindings are not fixed at the heel, enabling the skier to slide the ski forward with a fluid, rhythmic motion, the heel lift providing more momentum.

Nearly all ski resorts have cross-country ski trails, which are clearly marked on the piste map. They tend to wind through quiet, attractive areas, and are set aside specifically for cross-country skiers to enjoy.

'Cross-country skiing is how skiing first began, and was originally a way of getting from A to B in flat, snowy countries before it became a recreational pastime.'

Alpine ski touring

Ski touring is a method of moving through the winter mountains using manpower, rather than ski lifts. This is a great way to get off the beaten track into areas that ski lifts don't service, to enjoy the untracked powder that most skiers can't get to. It's also a technique that a lot of mountaineers use to access winter routes – strapping the skis to their packs when they start climbing.

The skis used in ski touring are similar to those used in downhill skiing – but the bindings differ. Ski touring bindings have unfixed heels, similar to cross-country skiing, for when moving across flat or uphill terrain. However, the bindings are specially adapted so that the heel can be clipped back in, providing a more traditional downhill set-up for riding down steeper sections.

To aid the skier in the uphill sections, special ski touring 'skins' are attached to the base of the ski, ideally cut to fit the shape of the ski. Traditionally these were made from shorthaired animal skin, hence the name, but are now made from synthetic materials. The artificial skin consists of fine hairs, all smoothed in one direction. These are attached to the base of the ski with all the hairs pointing smoothly towards the tail end of the ski, so when the ski slides forward there is no obstruction to its movement. However, the ski struggles to slide backwards due to the fine hairs being pushed against the direction they're lying in, creating friction with the snow's surface. This enables the skier to go uphill without sliding back down.

When the skier reaches the top, they can easily remove the skins from the base of their skis, set their bindings to downhill mode and head off down the mountain – enjoying pristine snow, untouched by fellow skiers who have not made the extra journey off the beaten track.

Split snowboards

To enable snowboarders to share in the ski touring action, a snowboard was designed that can be split into two halves – the bindings are then rotated into a forward position and skins are attached to each half, enabling the rider to use them like touring skis, one half of the snowboard on either foot. At the top, the two halves are clipped back together again to reform one whole snowboard, and bindings are rotated back into a traditional snowboard stance, enabling it to be ridden downhill as though nothing had ever happened.

In theory, these are a good idea, but the jury is still out on the effectiveness of the 'skis'. There have also been tales of the clips on the specially adapted bindings snapping on various occasions.

Snowblades

Snowblades are essentially just very short skis. And when I say short, I mean really short – less than one metre. They are manoeuvrable, lightweight and designed for playing around.

Due to their size, they're easy to jump with and spin, and very nippy around the piste. However, take them off piste into the powder and you'll sink like a stone, due to the lack of substantial surface area to keep you afloat.

Although great fun, I think it's fair to say they do not have the best reputation, and are definitely not the coolest thing to be seen on. But if you think your reputation can survive a day playing around on these things, then what the heck, go for it – you'll probably have a great time.

Snowshoeing

As with cross-country skis, snowshoes also originated as a practical way of getting around in countries with long, cold, snowy winters.

Traditionally, a snowshoe looks like a large tennis racket, one for each foot, with your foot strapped to the centre. Modern day snowshoes have kept the similar shape, but have evolved to be more durable. The aim of the snowshoe is to enable you to hike through snowy areas without sinking up to your knees, which is exhausting. The increased surface area of the lightweight snowshoes keeps you on top of the snow, rather than in it, enabling you to get around far easier.

Snowshoeing is a wonderful way to get out into the mountains and enjoy the environment, especially if skiing or snowboarding is not your thing. There are plenty of tracks around, and the resort office will be able to recommend suitable trails for you to take.

It's possible to hire snowshoes in resort from most equipment rental shops. Ski poles are helpful for balance in the snow. If you do find yourself on a section of piste with skiers and boarders hurtling down, make sure you keep to the edge so as not to risk getting in their way.

Tobogganing

'Snowshoeing is a wonderful way to get out into the mountains and enjoy the environment, especially if skiing or snowboarding is not your thing.'

Now, I don't need to tell you what tobogganing is do I? If you haven't been able to bring toboggans out with you then worry not, lots of the equipment hire shops will rent them out to you.

Once the lifts have shut, hiking a short way up one of the beginner slopes that come down into resort, with your toboggan in hand, can be a fun way to spend an evening.

Some resorts even flood light the lower parts of a piste at resort level at night for this very reason.

Summing Up

- Cross-country skiing is a good way to get away from the crowds and enjoy the scenery of the mountains.

- For those of you who want to get off the beaten track, Alpine ski touring can get to areas not serviced by the ski lifts.

- Although they are not the coolest things to be seen on, snowblades are fun for jumping and spinning.

- Snowshoeing is a great alternative if skiing and snowboarding are not for you. It's also a great way to enjoy the mountain environment.

- Many resorts are happy for you to toboggan once the lifts have shut for the day – a fun way to spend an evening!

Help List

Air Travel Organisers' Licensing (ATOL)

www.caa.co.uk
ATOL is a financial protection scheme for holidaymakers. The scheme ensures that people do not lose their money should an ATOL contracted tour operator fail.

Bulgaria Ski

www.bulgariaski.com
Information on the Bulgarian ski resorts can be found on this website.

BUNAC

www.bunac.org
BUNAC offers a range of working abroad programmes. You can find information on working ski seasons in Canada and the USA on their website.

Chalet Finder

www.chaletfinder.co.uk
A website showing self-catered chalets for rent all over Europe and the US.

Chilean Ski

www.chileanski.com
A Chilean tour operator with good information on the resorts.

Chill Factore

www.chillfactore.com
Chill Factore is Manchester's real snow centre. You can choose from lessons, development sessions or just a practice. See their website for details of opening times and prices.

Club Med

www.clubmed.co.uk
Offering all-inclusive ski holidays, in 80 resorts across the world, for families and couples.

Crystal Ski

www.crystalski.co.uk
Ski and snowboarding holidays, in a range of accommodation across Europe, US, Canada and Japan. One of the largest tour operators in the UK.

Decathlon

www.decathlon.co.uk
Sporting goods emporium, offering a wide range of both well known and own-brand products at competitive prices.

Edge2Edge

www.edge2edge.co.uk
Edge 2 Edge are a ski and snowboard hire shop, based near Gatwick Airport. You can also buy ski and snowboard equipment from them as well as hiring.

Ellis Brigham

www.ellis-brigham.com
Ellis Brigham specialise in outdoor clothing and equipment. Check the website for details of their UK stores.

Erna Low

www.ernalow.co.uk
Ski specialists since 1932, offering ski holidays and accommodation in France, much of Europe and North America.

First Choice Ski

www.firstchoice-ski.co.uk
Tour operator offering affordable skiing and snowboarding holidays for families across Europe.

Headway

www.headway.org.uk
Headway is the brain injury association – they have campaigned in the past for legislation to make helmets compulsory for skiers and snowboarders.

Ifyouski.com

www.ifyouski.com
Cheap ski holidays in France, Austria, Italy, Switzerland, Canada and USA, from chalet holidays to hotel deals. Website also includes resort guides, gear and technique information, ski jobs and ski resort properties for sale.

Igluski

www.igluski.com
Ski deals on ski chalets, family skiing and luxury chalets. Plus ski resort information and snow reports. Features holiday deals specifically aimed at beginner skiers and snowboarders.

Inghams

www.inghams.co.uk
Tour operator offering ski and snowboarding holidays through out Europe and in the US. Catering for all budgets and groups.

Lonely Planet

www.lonelyplanet.com
A great source of general information about each country in the world.

Mark Warner

www.markwarner.co.uk
Chalet, and chalet-hotel ski holidays to France, Italy and Austria. Option to book adult only holidays.

Marks and Spencer

www.marksandspencer.com
Marks and Spencer sell a good range of thermal under garments, as will most high street department stores.

Natives.co.uk

www.natives.co.uk

Natives.co.uk is a website dedicated to seasonal ski working – you can find information about jobs, resorts, training courses, news, events and snow updates. It is run by ex-seasonal workers and contains a wealth of knowledge for anyone wanting to get into seasonal ski working.

Neilson Ski Holidays

www.neilson.co.uk

Tour operator offering ski and snowboard holidays across Europe, Canada and the US, in apartments, chalets and hotels.

Rough Guides

www.roughguides.com

Another good source of general country information.

Scott Dunn

www.scottdunn.com

Exclusive holiday provider, offering luxury ski holidays across Europe, the US, Canada and even Chile.

Ski Club

www.skiclub.co.uk

A skiing information site covering hundreds of ski resorts.

Ski France

www.skifrance.co.uk

A website where you can find lots of information on the French resorts. You can buy ATOL protected package holidays through this website.

Ski Norway

www.ski-norway.co.uk

Information on the ski resorts in Norway and how to book your holiday.

Ski Scotland

http://ski.visitscotland.com
The official snowsports website for Scotland. Check the site for snow conditions and information on skiing in Scotland.

Ski Total

www.skitotal.com
Tour operator offering ski package deals to Austria, France, Italy and Switzerland.

Skiworld

www.skiworld.ltd.uk
Tour operator offering a huge range of ski and snowboard holidays, in a range of accommodation from luxury to budget, across Europe, the US, Canada, Japan and South America.

The Snow Centre

www.thesnowcentre.com
The Snow Centre is in Hemel Hempstead and is Britain's newest real snow centre. You can do lessons or just go for a practice. See their website for details of opening times and prices.

SnowDome

www.snowdome.co.uk
The SnowDome in Tamworth, Staffordshire is an indoor real slope. You can do lessons, coaching sessions or just go for a practice. See their website for details of opening times and prices.

Snow Japan

www.skijapanguide.com
A good source of information if you're thinking of going further a field for your skiing holiday.

Snow+Rock

www.snowandrock.com

Snow+Rock is a specialist outdoor clothing and equipment store. Check the website for details of their UK and Ireland stores.

SNO!zone

www.snozoneuk.com
SNO!zone operate three indoor real slopes in the UK: Milton Keynes, Castleford and Braehead in Scotland. You can take lessons or just go for a practice. See their website for details of opening times and costs.

Thomson Ski

www.thomsonski.co.uk
Tour operator offering a range of good quality ski and snowboard holidays across Europe, Canada and the US.

TK Maxx

www.tkmaxx.com
TK Maxx is a cut-price retailer who have a range of ski and snowboard clothing. See their website for details of their UK stores.

Welcome Argentina

www.welcomeargentina.com
This website has good information about skiing in Argentina.

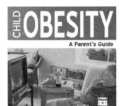